Edgar H. [from old catalog] Kellar

Lessons In Soul-Winning

Edgar H. [from old catalog] Kellar

Lessons In Soul-Winning

ISBN/EAN: 9783741134265

Manufactured in Europe, USA, Canada, Australia, Japa

Cover: Foto ©Thomas Meinert / pixelio.de

Manufactured and distributed by brebook publishing software
(www.brebook.com)

Edgar H. [from old catalog] Kellar

Lessons In Soul-Winning

Motto: "FISHERS OF MEN."

LESSONS IN SOUL-WINNING,

WITH SPECIAL REFERENCE TO

HOUSE TO HOUSE VISITATION.

BY E.

Secretary of the Evang   *unday-school*
Un

CHRISTIAN

TABLE OF CONTENTS.

INTRODUCTORY. - - - - - - 6

PART I.

THE WORK EXPLAINED.

Lesson 1	Outlined.	The Initiatory Step	- -	13
"	2	"	Delicacy of the Work	- -	18
"	3	"	The (House) Home	- -	21
"	4	"	How to Gain Access — House-to-House	- - - -	23
"	5	"	How to Use the Cards	-	26
"	6	"	How to Consider the Poor—the Rich	42
"	7	"	How to Approach the Unsaved	-	45
"	8	"	Concerning the Parents	-	48
"	9	"	The Young People	- - -	51
"	10	"	The Children	- - -	53
"	11	"	The Foreigner	- - -	56
"	12	"	The Negro	- - -	59
"	13	"	The Roomer—Boarder	- -	60
"	14	"	God's Plan	- - -	63
"	15	"	The Fraternity Settlement	-	66

PART II.

THE WORKER QUALIFIED AND EQUIPPED.

I. QUALIFIED.

Lesson 1	Outlined.	Confidence	- - -	73
"	2	"	Courtesy	- - - -	76
"	3	"	Consecration	- - -	78
"	4	"	Incentives	- - - -	80
"	5	"	Opportunity and Adaptability	81
"	6	"	Prayer	- - - -	86
"	7	"	Personal Cautions	- -	88

(3)

II. Equipped.

Lesson 8 Outlined.	Knowledge of the Scriptures	-	90
" 9 "	Knowledge of Mankind	-	92
" 10 "	What Sin Is	- - -	94
" 11 "	Know Doctrines	- -	97
" 12 "	Judgment	- - - . -	101
" 13 "	Principles of Imparting Faith		103

PART III.

THE KINGDOM OF GOD.

Lesson 1 Outlined.	The Kingdom as Described by Jesus - - - -	107
" 2 "	How the Apostles Made Disciples	110
" 3 "	Organization - - -	113
" 4 "	The Visible and Local Congregation - - - -	118
" 5 "	Things Done to Build Up the Congregation - - -	120
" 6 "	Relations of Congregations to Each Other - - - -	122

PART IV.

DISOBEDIENCE EXAMINED.

Introduction to Part IV. - - - - 127

SECTION A.—THE SUPERFICIAL.

1. Lack of Deep Conviction - - - -	128
2. "Still a Little Skeptical" - - -	129
3. "Wait Until a More Convenient Time - -	130
4. Love of Ease - - - - -	132
5. Not "Called" Yet - - - - -	132
6. Controversial Spirit - - - -	134
7. "Won't Believe what I do not Understand" -	134

SECTION B.—THE APOSTATE.

8. (1) "Cannot Hold Out" - - - -	137
9. (2) "Tried Without Success" - - -	138

10. (3) Inconsistencies of Christians -   -   140
11. (4) "Too Great a Sinner" -   -   -   -   140

SECTION C.—THE BEWILDERED.

12. (1) The Superstitious -   -   -   -   143
13. (2) Spiritual Blindness—Ignorance -   -   -   144
14. (3) Too Great Regard for Human Traditions -   145

SECTION D.—COMMENDING THEMSELVES.

15. (1) Love of Praise -   -   -   -   -   148
16. (2) Fear of Man -   -   -   -   -   148
17. (3) Not Willing to Leave Impenitent Associates - 149
18. (4) "Don't Like the Messenger"   -   -   150
19. (5) Insincerity -   -   -   -   -   -   151

SECTION E.—FOES WITHIN AND WITHOUT.

20. (1) Too Many Things to Give Up   -   -   153
21. (2) Pride of Birth -   -   -   -   -   154
22. (3) "Too Smart" -   -   -   -   -   155
23. (4) "Love of the World"   -   -   -   -   155
24. (5) Love of Money -   -   -   -   -   156
25. (6) "Cares of the World"   -   -   -   -   157
26. (7) "Don't Want Sins Exposed -   -   -   158
27. (8) Murmuring Spirit -   -   -   -   -   158

SECTION F.—THE SELF-RIGHTEOUS.

28. (1) "Don't Want to Confess Christ"   -   -   160
29. (2) "Don't Want to be Baptized"   -   -   -   162

SECTION G.—MANY INFALLIBLE PROOFS FOR THE
UNBELIEVERS.

30. (1) Theories of Infidelity -   -   -   -   165
31. (2) Internal Evidences   -   171
32. (3) External Evidences   -   176

INTRODUCTORY.

AFTER MANY YEARS.—It is quite apparent that Christianity must be reduced, as far as possible, to a science, and its truths be applied, in a catholic way, by trained soul-winners for the coming of the Kingdom in its fullness.

AN EFFORT TO ORGANIZE, EDUCATE AND UTILIZE.—The Sunday (Bible) School movement is a successful effort to utilize the sentiment generated in the Church by the Gospel to care for, especially, the children of Church members. This movement is on an interdenominational and catholic basis.

The Young People's Society of Christian Endeavor fills a similar place in the utilization of sentiment to care for the young people of the Church, with an eye to a universal sweep, and without antagonizing denominationalism.

Now there is a vast sentiment—a dominant missionary idea—that reaches out after the children, the young people, the parents, who are without the blessings of Faith.

Especially adapted for city conditions, yet knowing neither denominational nor territorial bounds—mark it!—these systematic lessons in soul-winning are a humble effort to *organize, educate* and *utilize* this sentiment.

THINK ON THIS!—''And thus also the furtherance of God's Kingdom, both in general and in
each individual community, the furtherance of
the propagation of Christianity among the heathen, and the improvement of each particular
Church, was not to be the concern of a particular chosen class of Christians, but the nearest
duty of every individual Christian.

''Every one was to contribute to this object
from the station assigned to him by the invisible
Head of the Church, and by the gifts peculiar to
him, which were given to him by God, and
grounded in his nature—a nature which retained,
indeed, its individual character, but was regen-
erated and ennobled by the influence of the Holy
Spirit.

''There was no division into spiritual and
worldly, but all as Christians, in their inward
life and dispositions, were to be men dead to the
ungodliness of the world, and thus far departed
out of the world; men animated by the Spirit of
God, and not by the spirit of the world.''—*Nean-
der's History.*

WORDS OF THE NAZARENE.—''The harvest truly
is great and the laborers are few.'' ''Go.''
''Pray.'' ''Teach.'' ''Observe.'' ''I am
with you.''

SOUL-WINNERS' TRAINING (CLASSES—COLLEGE)
IN CONTEMPLATION.—All pastors and thoughtful
Christians view, with deep gratitude, the ad-
vances in the direction of *training* soul-winners

made by the Young Men and Young Women's Christian Associations, Christian Endeavor and kindred societies, the Sunday (Bible) School and the Church, although, so far as we know, there is not, nor has there been, any general, widespread or systematic effort in this direction.

DEVELOPMENT.—It is only a further development of this same dominant missionary idea that suggests a training-class in every Church, that there may be those, who are not only willing, but competent to do personal work.

There is a demand for this work, not alone, during the season of special revival, or in the various regular services of the Church, where the Christian and non-Christian may be thrown together, but for those trained fishermen, who will cheerfully subject themselves to the discomfiture and uncertainty of angling in unseen depths, who will go from one place of rendezvous to another, continually and persistently, braving sneer and insult, because on fire with the faith that such of mankind as are not brought into the Kingdom of the Living God are lost!

If one can be a storage-battery for God, outside the ranks of the faithful and within the enemies' enclosure, what could he not be and do, when all around are friends, and the atmosphere and surroundings are surcharged with Christian power?

THEREFORE, as the greater comprehends the lesser, so it is recommended, that this training-class of soul-winners be organized and instructed with special reference to fitness for house-to-house visitation.

ORGANIZE by the pastor, or any one sufficiently interested, calling a meeting of those who will be party to some such agreement as this.

COVENANT.—I, ..., believe that ''the kingdom of God and his righteousness,'' constitute the supreme interest of mankind in general, and myself in particular. Hence I do, hereby, enter into this solemn covenant to fit myself for personal work—soul-winning.

THE COURSE OF STUDY. — Besides common sense, a good English education, and a pure heart, it is expected that members of this class shall have been as well grounded in the knowledge and use of the Holy Word as the Church affords opportunity, in the present development of her activities. And beyond this,

THE BIBLE is to be carefully and systematically studied, with special reference to soul-winning. (Normally, it can be studied in no other way, but we are so blinded by selfishness.) And then,

THIS LITTLE BOOK, it is hoped, will be taken as a kind of manual in the attempt to adapt the truths of the Scriptures to the exigencies of our day, especially in house-to-house work; and so, anything that can be used to advance this purpose should be added; not, however, so as to make the course too extended or complex.

THE LEADER.—To develop independence, rapidity, and conciseness, patience, tact, and delicacy of thought and expression, let the members of the class alternate in leading.

MANNER OF CONDUCTING THE CLASS-MEETING.— Let the leader conduct a review of the previous lesson (with closed books and absence of notes), and the same leader, by lecture or conference, establish well the salient points in the next lesson. Thus, after the manner of lectures at college.

Let the leader and lesson-subject be selected and announced one meeting in advance. The use of the blackboard is recommended

ORDER OF EXERCISES (SUGGESTED).

1.   Scripture Reading—selected with reference to lesson to be reviewed.
2.   Hymn—selected with reference to lesson to be reviewed.
3.   Review of the previous lesson.
4.   Sentence-Prayer—by every member of the class.
5.   Study of the next lesson.
6.   Selection of leader and lesson. Miscellaneous.
7.   Hymn—Benediction.

PRAYER.—O our Father, dependent on Thee are we—on Thee alone. Grant to us humility. May we be free from any feeling of self-sufficiency. What have we that we have not received from Thee? O Thou art the Giver of all good! Blessed be Thy Holy name! Grant to Thy children zeal, constancy and wisdom. May we be altogether dominated, as was Jesus, by the idea of *service* to Thee and humanity, that Thy will may be done on earth as in Heaven. For Christ's sake. Amen.

PART I.

THE WORK EXPLAINED.

LESSONS IN SOUL-WINNING.

LESSON I. OUTLINED.

THE INITIATORY STEP.

DEVOTION.

O our Heavenly Father, help us to remember our covenant with Thee and among ourselves. May we be mindful that we are parts of a tremendous whole —that Thou art no respecter of persons, loving all alike—that we are to work together, so Thy great purpose in creating man may be fulfilled. We thank Thee for the measure of co-operation already attained; grant us grace to go on to greater things. For Jesus' sake. Amen.

ELABORATION.

Vast numbers in the great cities—probably not less than three-fifths—are renters; and this great number are, more or less, continually shifting from this house to that, from one part of the city to another. Moreover, many hundreds and thousands are annually added to the city's population—people moving in from elsewhere. Families are created every year by marriage, which go to housekeeping. All this makes it a matter of great urgency to get out a new directory annually, Business men understand this. The churches need a new directory with even a greater need; the haphazard, overlapping, irresponsible, unreliable way of the past is entirely inadequate—a relic of an anti-missionary, anti-co-operative age. When the preacher says, occasionally, from the pulpit, "If any of you know of any family or person in the neighborhood whom I ought to visit, with the view of having them become identified with us in our church, please let me know;" and the superintendent says, "Now let every scholar bring a new scholar next Sunday;" and, maybe, the enthusiastic pastor, when he enters upon his city charge, writes a fervent article for his denominational paper, in which he says, "Breth-

ren (to his fellow-pastors and elders), if
any of your members move to our city,
drop me a note with their addresses, so I
can look them up; oh! so very, very many
are lost every year to our churches in this
way." And that is about all there is of
it. Soon the preacher's hands are so full
with other matters that he cannot even
find time to look up the names that are
handed or sent him. As a next step, a
visiting committee is organized by the
Presbyterian pastor, and ten city blocks
are canvassed with reference, solely, to
his own congregation. The M. E. Church,
on the opposite corner, goes on a similar
hunt over about the same ten blocks.
The energetic superintendent of the Presbyterian Sunday-school organizes a movement to secure the children in ten blocks
for his Sunday-school; the superintendent of the M. E. school is impressed in
about the same way; and thus and so it
goes. Well, everybody is tired and dis-
gusted—those visited and those who visit.
Such house-to-house visiting is a conspicuous failure; even worse, in many in-

stances, working a positive injury, in that
(a) it causes certain of the visited to
attach undue importance to themselves;
(b) it leaves an impression of unbecom-
ing rivalry; (c) these flashes leave an impression of inconstancy and insincerity—
great attention for a short time, and then
absolute neglect; (d) some sections of
the city worked to death, and others altogether ignored. Moreover, in the local
congregation there is often no concerted
action; the Church acts without reference
to the Sunday-school, and vice versa;
and the Young People's Society is liable
to act independently. All this is to be
deprecated. The system we advocate
looks to thoroughness, co-operation and
efficiency, in the initial visit of the year—
concerted action, on the part of the local
church, and sister churches of all denominations. The initial visit is to locate
those unidentified with Christian work,
and to ascertain what denomination could
best enlist them. To divide the family
up—the father to this church, the mother
to that church, and the children to the

other church—is not the ideal condition; but such inharmony will, however, adjust itself, as denominations come to see eye to eye, which latter condition this movement will assist to effect.

The initial visit does not stand alone; it is the first, and differs somewhat from the following; but by no means is it an end of the matter. The initial visit means *every* house, *every* family, *every* person. Very much depends on the beginning; other people are to enter into our labor, even as we enter into theirs.

APPLICATION.

Do not display any bigotry or sectarianism whatever. Do *your* work *well*. In a sense, more depends upon the initial visit than upon any other. It means a concerted action on the part of Christian people, with absolutely no regard for denominational lines. You are to ascertain facts, interested only as a Christian.

In the "following up" visits, denominational channels may be used. *Remember* you are to work with the dominant

2

idea of the Church as a unit, not with un-
seemly rivalry of parts, but as one solid
and aggressive phalanx moving on to universal conquest and universal peace.

LESSON II. OUTLINED.

DELICACY OF THE WORK.

DEVOTION.

O Father of Wisdom, take now our
heads and hearts, acquaint us with a
sense of the fine, sensitive character of
this work, and free us from rudeness and
presumption. May we have the mind of
Jesus in seeking out and caring for the
stray. In His name. Amen.

ELABORATION.

That the work is too difficult and delicate is *not* a good excuse for declining to
make the effort; but, on the contrary,
should incite us. Whether we work or
refuse, an influence is set in perpetual
motion.

It is largely a question of grace in approach and in contact:

(a) Not on a parallel with an agent or canvasser, who has a more or less selfish motive in calling; but per contra.

(b) Not a quality to be attained without thought or exercise; but per contra.

(c) The ambiguity of speech adds difficulties to the work. Many delicate inquiries are necessary, sometimes, to establish one point clearly. To be brusque would be to court defeat.

(d) Once let the visited repose confidence in the visitor, and the remaining part is easy.

Extreme sensitiveness may arise from, (1) great selfishness, (2) deep sense of ignorance, (3) secret sins and fear of exposure, (4) confidence misplaced, (5) shattered hopes—in a word, here is *sin*, a great sore, inflamed and sensitive! O, the shattered nerves, the guilty consciences! O, the reckless, despairing, desperate souls! Yes, it is a delicate task to snatch the brands from the burning. No outside glamour of respectability or composure

should deceive. Let there be honest
diagnosis!

APPLICATION.

Go, be not faint-hearted; be dependent
on God's wisdom, not your own. Jesus
to the sinners, not to the righteous—be a
follower of Him in deed and in truth. Be
patient and sympathetic—don't pose as
some great one, you are not; take off your
gloves, it is fine work; lay aside the conventional flatteries and deceits. We
mean business and have no time for
trifling; take insult at nothing. If sneer-
ed at and reviled, stand it patiently;
Jesus did not revile again, be sure we do
not. Be loving; if love does not win, be
sure severity cannot. Be content with
little or no apparent progress; remember
you are sowing the seed. We do not sow
and reap the same day; remember, however, that with some souls the reaping
time is at hand; seek then for definite
committal. Do not lose your head; if
you are getting disconcerted and out of
sorts, withdraw a little while and pray;

or, where you are, just think a prayer. Avoid disagreements, or discussions of differences; attempt rather to build up a higher understanding by considering things upon which you can agree; thus, sympathy is shown and confidence is begotten.

LESSON III. OUTLINED.

The (House) Home.

DEVOTION.

O our Father in Heaven, we are grateful for the home on earth; help us to give to it purpose, and to grasp its associated ideas as it relates to others—obligations, responsibilities, hopes and fears—to the end that souls may be won. For Jesus' sake.

ELABORATION.

I. Consider its universality and evolution; the first and last abode of living man—the corollary of the family idea; corollary, from "corolla," a crown, and crown means to "dignify," "adorn," "complete;" hence, *home*, crown of the family, dignifies, adorns and completes it. Note the teleology of advance: cave, teepe, mud, log, modern house. Effects of civilization and Christianity, aspects of *exterior* and *interior*.

II. *The property idea* often represents a certain self-denial, one's own brain and brawn, sweat and blood. Where the heart is, there is the treasure also; undue attachment.

III. *Its title to respect*, because place of seclusion and of rest: Isa. 48: 22; Psa. 118: 165. O what words! And then its relation to religion, the family prayer altar—early prayers—the births, deaths, marriages.

IV. *Its soul and life* is in its influence on human life: joys, habits, sorrows, associations, etc.

APPLICATION.

We go into homes, not houses alone— go with the thought of what they may be (consider our ignorance), and what they should be (what Christ would have them). Not given to everybody to be "at home" with various classes. Can you? We have Divine Authority as well as human right to go, as gospel messengers, into *every* home (providing it is not resented). Don't doubt it.

LESSON IV. OUTLINED.

How to Gain Access—House to House.

DEVOTION.

O Thou, who providest abundantly every soul with every needed thing, grant us grace and knowledge to do Thy holy will. May we understand the manner of approach to each precious soul under domestic environment of all kinds. Grant to us the virtues of adaptability and taste and persistency, with the one object of soul-winning. For Jesus' sake. Amen.

ELABORATION.

Awkwardness, embarrassment, failure to adapt one's self to the occasion or surroundings, are always to be deprecated.

(a) *Time.* Select such times as will, most likely, be suitable to the class of people to be visited. As a rule, go between 9 and 11 A. M., 2 and 5 and 7 and 8 P. M.

(b) *Dress.* Dress with such taste as will, most likely, be free of offense and criticism to all classes. Don't underestimate this point.

(c) *Manner.* Be considerately cheerful and make it early apparent that you are not a canvasser or agent. If a servant answer the door, explain to him or her that your mission is one of friendliness and good will, avoiding the mechanical as much as possible; draw from her the information desired concerning herself, giving with kind words the invitation to church services; then ask her to carry a card to the householder (whose name you will have secured beforehand), with the request for a moment's conversation. Make it very clear that you are not out in the interest of any denomination, as such; that you are not to proselyte in that sense at all. Let it be understood, also, that you are not out soliciting alms for anybody or anything. In most cases a child or a woman will come to the door, and our first duty will be to disarm them of any suspicion. Act as though it were a neighborly call, and that is exactly what it is. Show no indication of displeasure or surprise whatever, at any sight, sound or smell that may assail you—you have no business to be proud or " stuck up " at any time, but especially would it be out of place in this work; don't give it up if you meet with silence and a cold stare— you are to expect just that sort of thing. A few more smiles and kind words will probably open the sealed lips; if you meet with rebuff or ridicule, stand it good-naturedly; the chances are it will not be repeated after the first snarl. Most people will receive you good-naturedly and many will be disposed to smile the thing off in an easy manner; be on your guard against such.

APPLICATION.

You are approaching your own brothers and sisters; be just as considerate and charitable and persistent as though, indeed, they wore your own name and were your immediate kin. Bear in mind that you are building for Eternity! be yourself a storage battery of Faith, Hope and Love.

LESSON V. OUTLINED.

How to Use the Cards.

DEVOTION.

O our Divine Father, grateful are we for all instrumentalities for the accomplishment of Thy holy will on earth; help us in our understanding of the means of co-operation and the plan devised to give efficiency and permanency to this work. We ask it in the name of Him who organized and sent forth the seventy and the twelve.

ELABORATION.

The Introductory and Invitation card:

(Should be of good card-board, about 2 1-2 x 4 in.)

"Whosoever Will, Let Him Come."

You are cordially invited to attend the services at the church of your choice

NEXT SUNDAY.

AND REGULARLY THEREAFTER.

This invitation is a general one, and is made by the Christian people of the city.

YOUR WELCOME IS ASSURED.

Presented by

REVERSE SIDE.

''The Spirit and the Bride say Come, and whosoever will, let him take of the water of life freely.''

''For God so loved the world, that He gave His only begotten Son, that whosoever believeth in Him should not perish, but have everlasting life.''

Be well provided with these cards. Insert your name before starting out. Use them freely, but not wastefully; they are all of some worth, and can be used at any time. It is intended to give *every* one, in this way, a personal printed invitation, and accompanied, if it be possible, with a spoken invitation. Be prepared to give location and other information of the principal churches in the city, and of all of every kind in the immediate neighborhood in which you visit. The following blank is suggested for the retention and exchange of information.

Each canvasser is provided with fifty of these slips fastened between card-board covers. On the front cover are blanks for the number of the district, name of canvasser, and a diagram on which the Chairman indicates the block to be canvassed by writing the names of streets about the diagram. At headquarters these books of slips are taken all apart and the slips fastened in packages according to denominations.

Name ....

Residence ....

	TOTAL.	Number Communicants.	Number Regular Church Attendants.	Not Attending Church.	In Sunday-School.	Not in Sunday-school.
Adults, 21 and over.....						
Youths, 4 to 20						
Under 4 years.............						
TOTALS						

Member of what church...

....

What denomination preferred..

....

....

Which branch of said denomination...

....

Visit advisable...(Yes or no.)

Remarks..

....

....

....

Each visitor is provided with a slip upon which are suggestions as follows:

SUGGESTIONS FOR VISITORS.

1. Undèrstand as thoroughly as possible the work expected of you, before you begin.

2. Let your dress and address recommend your religion.

3. Ascertain, if possible, the name of the family residing in the house before calling.

4. Use the utmost skill in your speech, remember that love alone wins.

5. As you enter, breathe a silent prayer for Christ's presence and help.

6. Write plainly. Miss no one. Get accurate information. Leave one invitation for each person.

7. Include all hired help and boarders, but under their own respective names, and on a separate blank.

8. Under "Remarks" note reasons for non-attendance, etc., state in one word any incident, comment or experience that may be striking.

9. Complete your work as soon as possible and report to your chairman.

10. Remember, the object of this co-operative and thorough canvass is not so much to do the work, as to point out to churches and Sunday-schools the work to be done afterward.

Do not mark, as for special visit, those who are in good standing and full fellowship in some one of our city churches; no cognizance should be taken of such (save in exceptional cases, where there is palpable neglect on the part of the church, the member being destitute, or sick, in special and sudden distress), any more than to enumerate the visit and number visited, etc., for it is to be supposed that all full members are enlisted for *work* in the Lord's army. Note, however, that one should inquire narrowly, but discreetly and courteously, into this matter, because heretofore many have reported in a brief, laconic way: " Yes, I am a church member," a " Protestant," or maybe, "Methodist" or "Baptist," without qualification or limitation, when, in reality, they only lean that way, or have been so reared, or their parents were such, or they themselves were such before coming into the city, or they think of becoming such some time, etc. Let us be on our guard in this matter.

A visit is advisable in every instance where the visited is *not identified* with any local congregation in the city, and who, needing, would not *resent* a visit from a friend. Be very accurate in writing down the name, address, etc.; don't approach a person with pencil and card in hand and demand the name and address, but after you have established sympathy, and determined the items desired, ask if the person has any objection to permitting you to write down a few points. If, however, you fear giving offense, retain the points in mind and insert them later. We are not governmental employes propounding interrogations mechanically, Remember!

DISTRICT CHAIRMAN'S REPORT.

District Number................

Number Canvassers...

Number visits made..

Total number visited..
Number adults—21 and over ....
Number youths—4 to 20...
Number under four years...
Number not attending church.......................................
Number in Sunday-school..
Number youths not in Sunday-school............................
Number attend neither church nor Sunday-school..............
Number having no preference...
Number visits advisable...

	Communi-cants.	Attend Regularly.	Prefer-ence.
Number Methodists			
Number Lutheran.........			
Number Christian....................			
Number Baptist			
Number Presbyterian..............			
Number Unitarian....................			
Number Jewish.....			
Number Episcopalian................			
Number Congregational...........			
Number Miscellaneous.............			
Number total Non-Catholics...			
Number Roman Catholics........			
TOTAL...................			

The suggested forms and blanks herein set forth are tentative. However, they have served for canvassers in St. Louis, Louisville, Kansas City and elsewhere. In St. Louis, where the author has been for some years Secretary of the House-to-House Board, new schools have been organized, and in some instances local congregations sprang into existence almost as the immediate result of the canvasses.

I spread upon the pages of this book the Secretary's "Salient Points," report made after the Fall canvass of 1893; the previous annual canvasses had been made in the Spring.

HOUSE-TO-HOUSE VISITATION—SALIENT POINTS.

1st. Activity in the interim. In many cases using the district boundaries as laid out by our interdenominational Board, but confined to local church channel, and practically ignoring other churches, near or far, thus sufficient in itself, and reluctant to go into the general movement.

2d. Denominational activity (*i. e.*, co-operation among churches of the same denomination), and so again averse to interdenominational co-operation.

3d. Disposition to give up the effort to secure sufficient and efficient volunteer help; but to pay for efficient service of one or two, and extend the time for several weeks.

4th. Pronounced indisposition to settle down to the good, hard work of the movement, both in the initiatory and the "following up" (not more noticeable this year than formerly, however, if the novelty of the movement be eliminated). This indisposition is shown by, (a) increased sensitiveness at rude treatment; (b) "don't like to interfere with the regular work of the Church;" (c) "don't do any good anyhow, because people are set in their ways;" (d) "it breaks into our denominational arrangements in this direction;" (e) information is refused because (it is said) the movement is in the interest of the "A. P. A."

ANSWER.—Doubtless we should con-

sider such indisposition thus: (a) If
rudely treated, let it not be the occasion
of cessation of endeavor, but rather induce patience and skill and persistency—
see life of Christ. (b) Regular routine of
church services permits many to slumber.
The orthodox Jewish services in the time
of Christ served to lull to ease and repose
great numbers of the Jews, who by an
outward conformity concluded they had
discharged the demands of the faith. (c)
"Nothing is settled until it is settled
right;" the *cui bono* is of the devil, and
obsolete in this relation, or else why
Christ at all? (d) Denominationalism
thus becomes the bane of Christianity; it
is anarchy, the haphazard, go-as-you-
please bigotry that retards the coming
Kingdom; for, "when one saith, I am of
Paul; and another, I am of Apollos; are
ye not carnal?" (e) The movement has
absolutely no connection whatever with
any secret society or political party.
Over a year ago it was suggested to divide
the city according to wards and precincts
for the purpose of comparisons of relig-

ious with political life. Leaving out of
consideration any purpose of comparisons, such division might have been acceptable, and was followed in our neighboring city, Louisville, but was avoided
here purposely to discountenance the
charge of being used for political purposes. The matter was laid before the
Board again this fall, and again defeated.

FAILED TO RECKON.—The committee
failed to take into account the Church as
a religious club, the pastors as overtaxed,
and the fact that the churches are so
dead in selfishness, coming from the summer's relaxation, as to need, aye, require,
the enthusiasm usually engendered in the
winter's work so as to set the people at
work to "compel them to come in." Our
vacation system in the city is at fault
somewhere; it takes nearly all winter to
regain what we lose in the summer. The
loitering school-boy takes three steps forward and two backward, and is tardy.

SATIATED WITH STATISTICS.—The past
canvasses have brought so much to light
in this respect that many stand appalled

and consider any reform movement a forlorn hope—so many have lost their aptitude (if, indeed, they ever possessed any) for soul-winning, and satisfy themselves (and not infrequently the preacher) by giving a genteel sort of service, a contribution in dollars, but not in personal duty performed in the presence and to the person of the worldly.

MANY HAVE GROWN TIRED.—After the novelty, after the flush of one great step taken, after the half defeat, after working up to the canvass again, and then again, after the churches were not filled and the Sunday-schools had not doubled their membership—then comes the "tired feeling." It is one thing to spy out the country, and quite another thing to take and hold it. One thing to co-operate for information, and quite another for ingathering.

SUPPOSE WE DO KNOW that in a given district there are 4,000 souls, 1,800 adults, 1,600 youth, and 600 under four years old. Only 200, or one-twentieth, are church members; 150, or one-tenth, of the youth in the Sunday-school (not reckoning Catholics); and these members and pupils divided up among a score of denominations? Rather serious condition, but what shall we do?

WHAT MORE TO DO.—Has not each home been visited and a printed card of invitation to attend divine services been given to all? Yes. But did they come? No—perhaps one or two. Were they then not assorted, and did not one specific congregation send out written or printed invitations to attend a specific service? Yes, in some few cases. And was there an encouraging response? No, they did not come in large numbers. Is it not true that there are churches and schools with conspicuously-hung signs, "All are welcome," where services are conducted regularly, and whose doors are open? And how many attend? Perhaps out of 4,000, 300 combined attend Sunday-school and church regularly, and another 300 occasionally. Well, what more can be done? *What more?* Why, it all remains to be done!

NOT ENOUGH.—Of course it is not enough to hand out a printed invitation; one might as well expect to have the house full by inserting a deftly-worded invitation in the newspaper. It is not enough, having learned the destitution spiritual and the predilection religious, to send a special invitation. No, it is not enough to hold out inducements of reward cards and such for attendance at Sunday-school. Nor will it suffice to have conveniently located churches, with attractive and conspicuous signs, "All welcome; seats free." Well, what then?

THE CHRIST HEART.—How true is it that religious clubs are exclusive, that the churches frequently do not care for increased usefulness! That genuine faith and repentance and obedience are rare and exceptionally fine conditions, and not acceptable to the mass of the people. The *grace that comes from God*, and not from man, to secure and to hold those outside. Alas! alas! the aptitude and love for soul-winning dwell in very few hearts.

HERE IS THE SUGGESTION FOR YOU.— *Pastoral Co-operation. Cottage Prayer- Meetings. Neighborhood Sunday-schools.* On this mundane sphere that army of the Lord, with no councils of war and. no communications between divisions and companies, is insane and foolish (if ultimate victory be honestly desired and expected.) This is our present condition. Who will deny it? Organize the St. Louis pastoral co-operation with auxiliaries in each of our eighty-one districts.

AUXILIARY CO-OPERATION.—(1) Organize with corps of officers that will include pastors and superintendents of all churches and Sunday-schools in the district. (2) Hold monthly meetings in rotation from one church to another. (3) Two elections annually. (4) Objects: (a) Keep religious directory of the district continually corrected; (b) Interchange of information and suggestions and studies in soul-winning—cottage prayer-meetings, neighborhood Sunday-schools; (c) Reports from pastors and superintendents as to increase in church and Sunday-school; (d)

Afford relief to the destitute; (e) Report twice a year to the Central Co-operation.

CENTRAL PASTORAL CO-OPERATION.—A joint organization of the Sunday-school Union and Alliance, something after the order of our present House-to-House Board, to secure desired uniformity, have general supervision of the movement, and keep the auxiliaries working, etc., "till all attain unto the unity of the faith, and of the knowledge of the Son of God."

LESSON VI. OUTLINED.

How to Consider the Poor—The Rich.

DEVOTION.

O our Divine Father, help us to hold in mind the teaching of Thy Word concerning these two great classes, that we may act rightly in any and all cases. Give us an eye to distinguish between the real and the apparent. We are deeply thankful for Thy providence of material things —we are unspeakably grateful for Thy

providence that freely gives unsearchable
spiritual riches to the humblest, the most
ignoble and ignorant, through Jesus,
who became poor that we might be rich.
Amen.

ELABORATION.

In Material Things.—Causes of poverty: *Good*—self-sacrifice, missionary
zeal. *Indifferent*—accident, sickness. *Bad*
—sloth, dissipation, evil associations,
gambling. Causes of riches: *Good*—
thrift, invention, economy. *Indifferent*—
inheritance, accident. *Bad*—gambling,
fraud, treachery, stinginess. The Scriptures further say: Riches are corrupting,
perishable, deceitful, unsatisfying, source
of envy and strife, lead to pride and
hard-heartedness and oppression and
sensuality, and the forgetting and forsaking of God. Moreover, those who possess
riches should not set their hearts on
them, or trust in them, or boast of them,
or glory in them, or hoard them up, but
rather ascribe them to God, devote them
to God's service, and make the poor par-
takers of them.

The vast majority are neither poor nor
rich; these terms are relative, flexible
and elastic. No moral quality necessarily
involved; consider the temptations and
sins that are liable to accompany ex-
tremes. Riches *never* an unavoidable condition; poverty may be: a rich man can
always give away his riches, but a poor
man *cannot always* dispose of his poverty. Envy, avarice and gross selfishness
not uncommon in the poor. The Christian desires immaterial riches, *i. e.*, treas-
ures above—this is *real* wealth; all men
should sacrifice riches for such. God is
no respecter of rich or poor. God owns
it all.

APPLICATION.

We must be affected by neither the one
nor the other condition; ignorance, vice,
infidelity and crime exist in both classes.
Appearances are not an indication. Do
not be guilty of one of the great sins of
our day, namely, *toadyism.* Salvation
from sin is found in Jesus Christ alone.
Riches save no one, and poverty damns

none. Strive to be *rich* in *good* works. "There is a burden of care in getting riches, fear in keeping them, temptation in using them, guilt in abusing them, sorrow in losing them, and a burden of account to be given up at last concerning them."—*Matthew Henry.*

LESSON VII. OUTLINED.

How to Approach the Unsaved.

DEVOTION.

O our Father, may we realize the wonderful truth—"By unbelief they entered not in;" "He that believes not shall be condemned." That we may be stirred up to our full duty, may we keep in mind the words, "If you love them that love you, what reward have you?" "If you salute your brethren only, what do you more than others?" We have been selfish and unchristlike; O forgive us! May we be like Jesus. We ask in His name. Amen.

ELABORATION.

Four kinds or attitudes of the mind and heart towards Christ:

(1) Convicted—those who want to be saved.

(2) Awakened—those who are interested.

(3) Careless—those who are indifferent.

(4) Rebellious—those who refuse to listen.

"Zeal without knowledge," "apathy," "inconstancy," might be written of a vast amount of the efforts to win souls in the past. The efforts, in the direction of personal work, put forth during seasons of revival, the zeal young Christians manifest, are not to be spoken of slightingly. Although the one is sometimes spasmodic, and the other sometimes without knowledge, it is far better than the lifeless "O won't you join our church, our minister is so nice?" of the apathetic. Special attention is required to efface these faults: (1) *Diagnosis*—analysis and synthesis, taking apart and putting together of elements in character, as heredity and environment and manifestation, the *enfolding* and *unfolding* of each life. (2) *Individual*—We have to do with an individual—a unit—not a class. One, however, who has lived in more or less touch with Christianity all his life; note, therefore, the *Geist Zeit*. We are not the first century disciples, with a gospel that is a novelty, to encounter the prejudices and superstitions of the polytheistic myths, the esoteric philosophy of Rome and Greece and Egypt. But we are dealing with an old, old story, after nineteen centuries of misapprehensions, encountering the perplexing vices of an heathenized Christianity—the same old gospel, overloaded with the rubbish of human traditions and misunderstandings. Shall we not be stouthearted and sink the true old gospel-blade down into the root of misrepresentation and the nineteenth century enormities? Let the burden of your counsel be, to the

Convicted: Trust and *obey.*

Awakened: Jesus is trustworthy.

Careless: Immortal soul accountable.

Rebellious: Reductio ad absurdum—
few words—a good example.

APPLICATION.

AVOID	CULTIVATE
Ostentation.	Observation without Impudence.
Flattery.	Sympathy without Softness.
Insinuations.	Humility without Hypocrisy.
Flippancy.	Seriousness without Gloom.
Censoriousness.	Fact without Intrigue.

LESSON VIII. OUTLINED.

CONCERNING THE PARENTS.

DEVOTION.

Our Heavenly Father, Thou hast sanctified the marriage relations; in Thy sight and economy the Family is at once school and sanctuary—we learn, we worship. O grant that all influences of parental life may be holy—that children may be reared in the nurture and admonition of our Lord. For Jesus' sake.

ELABORATION.

After entrance, do not stop to talk with the children, but speak to the point, with the parent; the parents control the children, and if you win the co-operation of the parents, you reach the children. Kindly assume the aggressive; judiciously defend the church. You can not waste time in listening to long tales of woe, or insidious attacks on the faith—look right into the eye with fullest candor. Press the following points home: You need the church, its music, its cheer, its society, its peace. Don't try to get " fit," *go as you are.* Keep continually sweet and cheerful, then—your children are growing a character. What are you willing to do about it? Are you fearful of bad influences? Consider the good influences of Sunday-school—may I enroll them right now? (Only a little plain, pleasant, pointed talk to the parent.) No expense attached (comparatively) to religion — think! Sunday-school literature, Sunday-school teachers' work gratis—funerals, visits free, good cheer—preacher's good advice cheap? Yes, cheap, like sun and air—but O how valuable! See! Prevents blues, dissipation, crime! Ah, it is the

4

Salt, the *Light!* And then pray, right
on your feet—short—to the point—no
cant or whine.

Have clearly in mind, believe what you
want to say, say it; when you are through,
go; don't dillydally about it—just go.
" God bless you !" open the door, and go
on about the Master's business. " The
King's business requires haste."

APPLICATION.

Secure the attention, win the co-operation. Don't underestimate the parent's
power and influence—exalt your work—
don't waste your time; yours is an inval-
uable opportunity. It took grace to get
into their house, let nothing of cowardice
or timidity or thoughtlessness defeat you
in accomplishing your purpose. Mid-
summer is a little late to sow the seed,
you might get in an after-crop, however.
In the main, cultivate the grace that may
be dormant within them—utilize it—get
all out of it you can, especially as it
relates to the children.

LESSON IX. OUTLINED.

THE YOUNG PEOPLE.

DEVOTION.

O our Heavenly Father, we thank Thee for the buoyancy of youth. Help us to understand its moods and whims, the melancholy of young manhood and womanhood, the chum-life, the loosenings of home ties, increasing responsibilities, and all the within and without that are so strange. Keep us ever in sympathy and touch with the young people, and may we win souls for Thee, our country and posterity. For Jesus' sake. Amen.

ELABORATION.

Now begin to show the individuality— every day brings some surprise. Under responsibility the dormant emotion, sensibility and will, seem to awake. Hold the reins gently but firmly—go the well-lighted road; in the dark paths disaster may occur before one is aware.

Study conditions of those from ten to twenty-five years, alone and in company, especially delicate matter to establish sympathy, as young people run to almost unaccountable chumships, and are sealed books to others. Study the magnificent proportions of responsibility, as the developer of character. Put the wavering, possibly selfish, physically strong, as guardian for a more delicately built and weak younger one (*a la* Tom Brown). Let all business for life be selected with a view to its possible effects on morals of the one so selecting. If this selection be permitted to go haphazard and slipshod, beware!

Recreations, entertainments and *amusements.* Fill the hours for such very full of the unquestionably right and proper, those that Jesus would allow, but withal, remember that life is a work-life, earnest, profitable, unselfish—be thrifty and shifty for the right always.

APPLICATION.

I may need my own advice. Have I not become *blase*, selfish, without conscious, independent strength? Is not this the

secret—in strengthening others I strength-
en self, in losing I find? O my soul, long
for earnest friendships, for a constant,
perpetual youth, with its hopes and vig-
ors and unimpaired enthusiasm. Live
and teach.

1. Keep good company or none.
2. Never be idle.
3. Live up to your engagements.
4. Keep your own secrets, if you have
any.
5. Never play at any game of chance.
6. Do not run in debt.
7. Be temperate in all things.

LESSON X. OUTLINED.

THE CHILDREN.

DEVOTION.

O our Father, we invoke Thy blessing
upon us as we enter on this great theme—
the children, whose angels are with Thee,
the children of whom Jesus spoke so frequently. May human depravity be met
and vanquished by the knowledge and

power of Godliness, in the earliest days
of infancy. O the little ones! how Thou
lovest them! how we love them! May
we be sensible and show our regard in a
practical way. To this end bless, we
pray Thee, the Sunday-schools and Young
People's Societies and the parents. For
Jesus' sake.

ELABORATION.

"Suffer little children"—all the child
needs is permission. The major part of
our most fruitful work lies in this direction. Paul to Timothy: "From a babe
(from infancy up) thou hast known the
sacred writings." So most frequently of
the faithful. The child born under the
most untoward circumstances, but reared
in God's grace, becomes a power for right
and conquest. Sow the seed in the
spring—train the tree in the green. O
the danger period—from ten to twenty!
Animalism, sensuality, overpowered with
tinsel and glare of this wicked world!
Actions that may set (become fixed) into
habits, and habits that may lead into hell!

The years from three to eight will likely tell life's tale, and fortify or weaken. God pity the youth, without compass or pilot, on life's ocean, on either hand the rocks—the whirlpool! There is no glory and little profit in saving a wreck. "Some men imagine they are forsaking the devil, when, in truth, the devil has only forsaken their worn-out bodies." Oh, the youth, the youth! our little loved ones, our hope, our promise and our power!

APPLICATION.

Drifting or guided? What am I doing about it? No notion of "original sin," or "infant baptism," should deter, swerve or mystify us as to our obligations to the children. Our Sunday-school could be increased a hundred-fold in attendance (and remain so), yes, and in efficiency and power, in one year. How? By the sensible, persistent efforts of us soul-winners from house to house. We deceive ourselves if we expect God to do what he has enjoined upon us. "God is

not mocked; whatsoever a man soweth,
that shall he also reap." God is helping,
and will help. "Bless the Lord, O my
soul, and forget not all His benefits."
And when, in the life of our youth, the
time comes when they must do for themselves what no one can do for them, O
may they have been so developed under
the influences of Godly environment that
all their actions may accord with the Holy
Will of God!

LESSON XI. OUTLINED.

THE FOREIGNER.

DEVOTION.

May we, O Father of all tongues and
every race, appreciate the opportunities
of our country, the health asylum of the
world, the world's hospital, that places
the stranger and foreigner in our midst,
and may all be assimilated into our
heaven-earthly government, a democracy
under Christ. O guide and preserve our
citizenship and studies in political eco-

nomics to this great end. We ask for
Jesus' sake.

ELABORATION.

What are we? God is no respecter of
persons. What, love the yellow, almond-
eyed, suspicious, treacherous Chinaman?
At a distance; we will send them mission-
aries. Love a "Dago," a dirty, dried-up
banana-peddler? Associate with him, be
a missionary to him? "It is impracticable; I haven't time; yes, it ought to be
done; their ignorance and anarchy might
wreck us; I will contribute a few dollars
for some one else to be the home missionary." Look out for this; it takes grace,
but God will give it; ask Him. The English tongue, not because it is English,
but as it is now the most universal speech
and the language of Christendom, carries
with it innumerable blessings. If you can
speak the foreign tongue, well and good;
if not, you can smile, act a real fraternity,
point to heaven. Remember the foreigner has left much behind him, and he
may leave his speech, also, if he be taken

with your kindness; convenience and love
will quickly help him to master our common tongue. It is but just, because the
discoveries and inventions and graces that
annihilate time and space, and make all
people one, demand one language—the
English. Let all come to it speedily. Of
course we may learn much from the Ger-
man, French, Russian, etc. Let us not be
conceited; our glorious composite under
Christ is not completed; but notice, like
Paul, we are debtors to all. Let us dis-
charge our obligations and Christianize
all.

APPLICATION.

The missionary districts in our large
cities should be shirked no longer. The
genius of our government demands that
we be *one*—acquainted and united; the
genius of our salvation requires the same
thing. To the work, then! Down with
the liquor business and gambling and kindred evils!

LESSON XII. OUTLINED.

THE NEGRO.

DEVOTION.

O our Heavenly Father, unspeakably grateful are we that world-wide emancipation moves on and on and on. In Thy grace no country like our own great democracy, with its millions of colored citizens, seems so advantageously situated to solve this race problem. Grant to us Christ-like grace and wisdom for this undertaking. Amen.

ELABORATION.

Harbor a sentiment, but not sentimentalism for the negro. The emancipation might come in a day, but the effects of slavery, with its commercial, social and religious complications, could not be eradicated in a day. It seems vain and foolish to make odious comparisons about cerebral superiority. The fifteenth amendment is doubtless just, and will meet with constantly increased favor. As far as opportunities and responsibilities go, let there be civil, commercial and religious equality before the law. Negro soul-winners may, from the nature of the case, work to most advantage among their own race. Expediency suggests a certain separation, while the common good requires a no inconsiderable amount of co-operation.

APPLICATION.

Our long continued and superior advantages should make us of especial great service to the negro, not in a patronizing way, but to assist them to lift the pall of superstition, immorality and ignorance that effects all races and peoples. Liquor, the intoxicating beverages, gambling and sensuality should be constantly deprecated.

LESSON XIII. OUTLINED.

THE ROOMER—BOARDER.

DEVOTION.

O our Heavenly Father, we come to Thee with our thanksgivings, our joys, our perplexities and our burdens. We need Thy wisdom and patience and grace in the matters before us. We so illy understand the great cities, the diversity, complications and temptations, bustle, business and small talk of hotel and boarding-house life. Help us to meet the situation gravely and seriously, and win it all for Thee and Thy kingdom. For Jesus' sake.

ELABORATION.

A fastly-increasing genus, with life and environment peculiar to itself—transient character—professional travelers, salesmen, actors, politicians, etc., etc. The regulars—clerks, railroad people, in business of all kinds, etc.—a life fraught with particularly dangerous environment, conducive to superficiality and selfishness.

The comforts of home are lacking. Comfort is sought in gambling, theater and bar-room and their adjuncts. Families boarding and children thus reared are subject to bad influences—neglected by churches. So many transients that come

to the city for a few days on business, or
pleasure, think nothing of throwing off
the restraining morals of their home, and
"going in to see the sights," demoralize
and debauch themselves, their city friends
and the municipality generally.

Think of club life as related to our subject—good, bad and indifferent, little and
big clubs, particularly abounding in city
life. The *"Institutional"* church is de-
manded to control and give direction to
such tendencies.

APPLICATION.

Why are theaters clustered "down
town," and not in the residence districts,
as are the churches? Among other reasons, a large number of their habitues
come from hotels and boarding-houses.
Does a large support of "turf ex-
changes," billiard-rooms, gambling-houses
and famous bars come from this homeless
genus? Are the homeless the godless?
If they are not, there is a strong current
setting that way. Are the godless the
homeless? Godlessness tends to home-

lessness. Has the church a work to do here? Aye, church homes for those whom business or misfortune render homeless. Soul-winners, bring them home.

God grant that the evening of sorrow may speedily close on all sin-soiled souls, and that the day-star of Christ's righteousness may flood such lives with light and love, with redemption complete, and all at home.

LESSON XIV. OUTLINED.

GOD'S PLAN.

DEVOTION.

O our Father, we believe that Thou art. Thy supreme sovereignty is unimpeached. We thank Thee that Thou hast shown us Thy will, Thy way, Thy word. May we have a clear vision and clean hands to see and handle this mighty matter. For Christ's sake.

ELABORATION.

Believe, know, feel, manifest and strive to convince all Christians that beyond a shadow of a doubt this personal interest in the individual soul, without respect to person, is God's plan. Go out into the highways, go out into the hedges, go out quickly into the streets and lanes of the city, into the mansions of the rich, the humble homes of the masses, the hovels of the poor. Go everywhere; continue to go, search diligently until every soul is found, and compel them, by love's gentle force, to come in. Said Jesus: "All authority is given me in Heaven and Earth. Therefore, *go*—go ye and make Christians of all, baptizing them into the name of the Father, and of the Son, and of the Holy Ghost, teaching them to *observe* all things whatsoever I have commanded you. And, behold, I am with you alway, even unto the end."

> "Her priests are all God's faithful sons,
> To serve the world raised up.
> O living Church, thine errand speed,
> Fulfill thy task sublime;

With Bread of Life earth's hunger feed;
Redeem the evil time.''

There are in existence an indefinite and large number of effective organizations for the purpose, in one way and another, of ameliorating the condition of humanity, of saving man. These are social, commercial, political and religious—local and general, denominational and undenominational and interdenominational. In a large and true sense the Church of God comprehends all.

BETTER AMALGAMATE.—This *diversity* is not to be especially deprecated; it is natural and right. These one thousand phases of work present themselves, and somebody must attend to each, and somebody will. It is the working of the Christ-leaven in the heart of man. Note, however, that we are only groping toward —have not attained that divinely enjoined condition of unity "where the whole body, fitly joined together and compacted by that which every joint supplieth, makes increase of the body in love."

5

APPLICATION.

Am I an operative Christian? The Lord of the harvest calls for laborers. Go fearlessly; cry, "Peace." "Salute no one on the way." No time for conventionalities. "Not eating from house to house." If the pleasure and purpose of acquaintance are only in feasting and conventionalities—Stop!

Do not call down fire because some fail to give credit to Christ.

LESSON XV. OUTLINED.

THE FRATERNITY SETTLEMENT.

DEVOTION.

Give, O Lord, grace to go and live among the lowly, that simple, honest life that proves by doing. Search us—are we self-righteous, sanctimonious, joined to an indulgence in enervating luxuries, or in the onward rush for dollars that shuts up our hearts of compassion? Have we a form, while we deny the power, of god-

liness? O may we present our bodies
holy—a reasonable service, transformed
by a renewed mind, to prove Thy perfect
will. For Christ's sake.

ELABORATION.

Our city Christianity—on the defensive
retreat system—abandon certain parts because given over to the poor renters—
poor but respectable—yet churches move
back. If the church were aggressive and
influential, the well-to-do would form set-
tlements among such, organize Institutional churches; it would **(1)** distribute
"the salt;" **(2)** give moral and financial
support to Christian work in such district; **(3)** act as a disinfectant for filth
and dirt; result in better sanitary conditions; **(4)** secure proper municipal pro-
tection and attention; **(5)** keep back
slum degeneration and kill it out; **(6)** induce simplicity and economy in living.
This is not slumming or rescue work. It
is real fellowship; not the long-range
dollar sort alone. *Affinity!* how can we
love? Determine, by God's help, to do

so, and then we can. What is influence
but the exercise of love—"Andrew goeth
and getteth Peter." Association good,
saves, as association bad, damns. So
many diffident and procrastinating—they
will warn one against the loss of money,
but not of soul.

Cannot be dogmatic in speaking of fraternity settlement. With rapid transit and
cheap fares all can live away from crowd-
ed tenement districts, and it is to be
hoped that such districts will soon be a
thing of the past.

APPLICATION.

Take greater interest in municipality—
not giving over certain districts to the devil
because the demon of poverty and shift-
lessness is approaching. It appears that
those well established in good character,
without children, or whose children are
grown, persons of influence and means,
ought to stay with the lowly and not run
away to city additions where there are
building restrictions—a kind of hermit-
like procedure. Stand for a full, round-

ed active church, a so-called Institutional church. The city presents certain ideal conditions—if it be a settlement of brothers it is heaven.

PART II.

THE WORKER QUALIFIED AND EQUIPPED.

SECTION I. QUALIFIED.

LESSON I. OUTLINED.

CONFIDENCE.

DEVOTION.

Our Heavenly Father, we are grateful for Thy thousandfold providences. With our weariness and woe there is rest nowhere but with Thee. O Thou infinite, all-powerful and all-loving One. May we turn from our wavering to Thy stability, our failings to Thy fulfillments. Thou art the "Yea and Amen" to all the Godward yearnings of our souls. O may we trust wholly in Thee and give Thee a full faith, a faith like Jesus'. In His name. Amen.

ELABORATION.

God in Christ is absolutely trustworthy. All secrets, all burdens, all temptations, all joys committed to God, (a) from youth; (b) with the whole heart; (c) all times; (d) under all circumstances.

(73)

Faith is "the substance" and "evidence" (Heb. 11: 1), or the "assurance" and "proving" (revised version). Necessary element of love—man's first duty. Win confidence—inspire to confidence by God's goodness. Gifts, power, sure promises, refuge, redeemer. If we trust we shall be kept "stable," "rejoicing," "inherit the earth," "fear not man," "enter into unsearchable riches." O consider God's faithfulness! Unbelievers "trust in man," "their own righteousness," "in wealth," "in vanity" and "falsehood." Confidence in God is *the* indispensable?

APPLICATION.

What hath God said? "Go, work," "win souls," inspire confidence, establish faith—without which God cannot be pleased and the soul's first need be met. Labor to inspire it everywhere, as we are in God's stead reconciling men, we must inspire the confidence of men in ourselves to win them.

We rise upon the eagle wings of Faith

to wind our way unto the happy heights, away, away, away above the woes and snows and throes of sin life; off, off, off unto the home of God, unto the very heights of everlasting Holiness.

THE RIFT OF THE ROCK.

‘‘In the rift of the rock He has covered my head,
  When the tempest was wild in the desolate land,
Through a pathway uncertain my steps He has led,
  And I felt in the darkness the touch of His hand
Leading on, leading over the slippery steep,
  Where came but the echoing sound of the shock,
And, clear through the sorrowful moan of the deep,
  The singing of birds in the rift of the rock.

In the rift of the rock He has sheltered my soul
  When at noonday the toilers grew faint in the heat;
Where the desert rolled far like a limitless scroll,
  Cool waters leaped up at the touch of His feet.
And the flowers that lay with pale lips to the sod
  Bloom softly and fair from a holier stock;
Winged home by the winds to the mountains of God,
  They bloom evermore in the rift of the rock.

In the rift of the rock Thou wilt cover me still,
  When the glow of the sunset is low in the sky,
  When the forms of the reapers are dim on the
      hill,
  And the song dies away, and the end draweth
      nigh.
It will be but a dream of the ladder of light,
  And heaven dawning near without terror or
      shock,
For the angels descending by day and by night,
  Will open a door through the rift of the rock.''

LESSON II. OUTLINED.

COURTESY.

DEVOTION.

Our Heavenly Father, we thank Thee
for the manifestation of those graces
that make Jesus so attractive and so win-
ning—faith, virtue, knowledge, self-con-
trol, patience, godliness and love,—O
Thine own attributes. Grant that all
may be blended into one and manifested
in our courtesy, our civility, so we may
be effective in soul-winning. We ask for
Jesus' sake.

ELABORATION.

Vaunteth not itself nor puffed up—not misbehaved; seeks not selfishly — not supersensitive.

"The more there is of a person the less likely is he to be fully known and understood by others." Then have consideration for all, for there is more of the most insignificant person than we are likely to fathom. It is easy to love those who love you, but there is no special grace nor salvation in that. We are after the lost, who do not love. Be courteous without expecting it in return; have patience and your courtesy will engender courtesy; let it be genuine, not conventional, nor forced.

APPLICATION.

Put yourself in the bewildered and lost soul's place; never be off your guard in any place at any time. Courtesy is the adaptability to circumstances — understand then this quality. Let it not lead you into compromise. Be firm but gentle, "For who among men knoweth the

things of a man, save the spirit of the
man, which is in him."

Courtesy is the essence of gallantry, the
badge of chivalry, the *sine qua non* of the
gentleman and the gentle woman.   Courtesy is not solely a deference, a negative
qualification; it is a defense, a loyal al-
legiance to the right.

"Some say that the age of chivalry is
past.   The age of chivalry is never past
as long as there is a wrong left unre-
dressed on earth, and a man or woman
left to say, 'I will redress that wrong or
spend my life in the attempt.'   The age
of chivalry is never past as long as men.
have faith enough in God to say, God will
help me to redress that wrong; or if not
me, surely he will help those that come
after me.   For His eternal will is to overcome evil with good."—*Charles Kingsley.*

LESSON III. OUTLINED.

CONSECRATION.

DEVOTION.

O Heavenly Father, we are Thine. Thy
service is our supreme joy, Thy Kingdom

is our delight, her walks our way, and her mansions our perpetual home! May we ever keep in the heavenly company of thy redeemed hosts, where we will praise Thee through Jesus Christ, world without end. Amen.

ELABORATION.

By consecration to God we more truly live than by our daily trades and vocations. We are redeemed, not by silver and gold. We are a peculiar people, not eccentric or erratic, but "dead unto sin," "alive unto righteousness," "a new creature in Jesus Christ," "a royal priesthood," "our brother's keeper."

What consecration *is not:* (a) Anxiety; (b) fault-finding; (c) censoriousness; (d) devotion to party; (e) or methods; (f) or traditions.

What Consecration is: (a) Graces; (b) purity; (c) devotion to Christ only, *i. e.*, not the only Christians, but Christians only; (d) a call; (e) a setting about for duty.

Consecration implies entire willingness, assurance, diligence, hospitality, blame-lessness, endurance, ministration, boldness, faithfulness, joy, obedience, charity, prayer, liberality, meekness, readiness, knowledge and zeal.

APPLICATION.

Christ contemplates every disciple as a reformer. " The history of the reformer, whether man or woman, on any line of action, is but this: When he sees it all alone he is a fanatic; when a good many see it, they are enthusiasts; when all see it, he is a hero."—*Frances E. Willard.*

Then what engagement has a Christian that is not comprehended and exercised in *soul-winning.* All the foregoing enumerated qualities and qualifications enter into this work. Soul-winning is fruit-bearing. " Whom wilt thou live for?"

LESSON IV. OUTLINED.

INCENTIVES.

DEVOTION.

O our Father, how glorious are Thy creations. How wondrously Thou dost sustain all with the stimulus of Thy incomprehensible Spirit. Grant that all our motives may find their prime and ultimate source in the Divine nature. We ask for Jesus' sake.

ELABORATION.

So many go through a round of eating, drinking and sleeping without motive, spur, stimulus, incitement or encouragement, save such as belong to the animal, viz., desire for ease and present gratification.

Fear of punishment and hope of reward are the two great factors in all human activity, and so arises another motive, viz., the desire for future gratification.

Our incentives are tried and trimmed, or new ones are born by our conceptions of our responsibility. Here comes in the *joy of service*, which is the complement of self-interest, making the wings upon which we scale the skies to glory. Rom. 2: 7, "To them that by patience in well-doing seek for glory and honour and in-

6

corruption, eternal life." Here are held
out three, aye, four things we all should
seek, the motor power of the civilized
world, "glory," "honor," "incorruption," and God, the righteous Judge,
rewards with "Eternal Life." Glory
means high reputation; honor means
office, position; incorruption means
purity, soundness. These are attain-
able conditions on earth. Mark it,
the necessary complement is, "seek by a
patient continuance in well doing," and
thus seeking, whether you succeed or fail
in securing reputation and office, you will
certainly have secured incorruption, and
God will crown you with everlasting success by giving you eternal life.

APPLICATION.

The possibilities of man under these
incentives are absolutely incalculable.
Let us go down into our bosoms—they are
ours, our very own—and, however dis-
agreeable, let us make a careful examin-
ation, and cast far from us, by the grace of
God, whatever is ignoble, vicious, or even

questionable in our motives. Let this
ruling ever ring in the heart and head,
"By a patient continuance in well-
doing."

WHAT DOES IT MATTER?

"'It matters little where I was born,
  Or if my parents were rich or poor,
Whether they shrank from the cold world's scorn,
  Or walked in the pride of wealth secure;
But whether I live an honest man,
  And hold my integrity firm in my clutch,
I tell you my brother, as plain as I can,
  It matters much!

It matters little how long I stay
  In a world of sorrow, sin and care;
Whether in youth I am called away,
  Or live till my bones of flesh are bare;
But whether I do the best I can
  To soften the weight of adversity's touch
On the faded cheek of my fellow man,
  It matters much!

It matters little where be my grave,
  If on the land, or in the sea;
By purling brook, "'neath stormy wave,"
  It matters little or nought to me;
But whether the angel of death comes down
  And marks my brow with a loving touch,
As one that shall wear the victor's crown,
  It matters much!''

LESSON V. OUTLINED.

OPPORTUNITY AND ADAPTABILITY.

DEVOTION.

We thank Thee, O our Father, for the myriad points of blessed contact with the infinite and the divine. Grant that we may ever be watchful and pliable in all that pertains to Thy kingdom. We ask for Jesus' sake. Amen.

ELABORATION.

Study the couplet,—

> "If you have anything to say,
> True and needed, yea or nay,
> Say it."

See how Jesus was an eternal example in this: (1) His patient obscurity; (2) baptism; (3) pointed and apt teaching; (4) character of his illustrations; (5) woman at the well; (6) Jesus and Peter —"Lovest thou me more than these?"

Wisdom to observe the one (opportunity) and employ the other (adaptability), is a great element of fitness. Paul calls it "redeeming the time;" and, if this be

done, every life, however ordinary, will
be full of testimony and blessing. Adaptability is a mark of genius, *i. e.*, godlike-
ness—firm but sympathetic, flexible but
immovable. "A bruised reed will He not
break, and a smoking flax will He not
quench."

APPLICATION.

You cannot see the opportunity until
too late? You can't adapt yourself? You
have tried? Are you willing to try, try
again? But you always fail? Are you
absolutely sure of that? No man knoweth; God knows.

ACCEPTED TIMES.

There are immortal moments in each life;
　　　They come and go—
One scarce may of their presence know,
Yet in them there is struck a chord,
It may be loud, it may be low,
　　　Of peace or strife,
　　　Of love or hate,
　　　Which will vibrate
Like circles from a pebble's throw,　　　,
Unto the coming of the Lord.
　　　　　　—*A. E. Hamilton.*

LESSON VI. OUTLINED.

PRAYER.

DEVOTION.

O our Heavenly Father, we thank Thee for the happy, holy communion of prayer —sweet hour—when Thy Spirit says to the troubled waters of our daily toil, "Be still." O teach us how to pray Thy will —Thy will be done; and to this end may we ever abide in Thee. We ask for Jesus' sake. Amen.

ELABORATION.

The prayer of faith is commanded, and should always be with obedience and without ostentation; with watchfulness but not anxiety. Always pray in the spirit of prayer, not the clamor of idle wants. Commune and give thanks in everything, and faint not.

Inquire—Is what I am going to say true? Is it useful? Is it kind? Hindrances: (1) Indulgence in sin; (2) Dimness of perception; (3) Inordinate cares.

You cannot reconcile prayer with God's immutable law. Law is God's method of work—not God nor his work. Without God law would fall. Thus government and law. In God's law provision is made for prayer. You say, yes, a general provision. If general, therefore special—not violent or contradictory. Comply with the conditions and your prayer will be answered.

APPLICATION.

Commune with God. O how it cheers and strengthens! It will give you God-like attributes, *i. e.*, courage, wisdom, self-denial and love. Pray with and for the disobedient. *Notice:* Prayer will often be the key to open the door in the obdurate heart for Christ's entrance.

DELIGHT THYSELF IN GOD.

Delight thyself in God,
Raise thou thine eyes above;
His heart is yearning o'er thee,
His bounty lies before thee,
Take thou thy fill of love.
The more thy need demands, the more will he
Extend the scepter of his grace to thee.

Delight thyself in God,
And all thou canst require

Shall be to him well-pleasing;
So will his love, unceasing,
Give thee thy heart's desire.
Pressed to his bosom, guided by his eye,
Thou wilt not ask the things he must deny.
                              —*Lucy A. Bennett.*

LESSON VII. OUTLINED.

PERSONAL CAUTIONS.

DEVOTION.

O what is man that Thou art mindful
of him? Forgive all our over-confidence
and boastfulness. O may our words and
works be forgotten and perish quickly if
they contradict Thy word and will. O
sustain us, or we fall and are undone.
We ask for Jesus' sake.

ELABORATION AND APPLICATION.

Say, with Paul, "Let him that thinketh
he standeth, take heed lest he fall." I
who have labored for others may be a
castaway. Am I a hearer only, thus
building on sand, and deluding myself?
Do I think myself religious while I bri-

dle not my tongue? Do I commit the
folly of measuring and comparing my
character with that of my acquaintances?
Do I keep myself unspotted from the evil
in the world, avoiding its very appearance? Have I been neglecting daily pri-
vate prayer and Bible reading? Do I
neglect the appointments of God's household?

Let me never believe what I feel if it
contradicts God's Word. Never under-
take a hazardous matter without asking
God's blessing and guidance. Never take
my Christianity from Christians, howso-
ever God may have used them, but from
Christ.

SECTION II. EQUIPPED.

LESSON VIII. OUTLINED.

KNOWLEDGE OF THE SCRIPTURES.

DEVOTION.

We thank Thee, our Father in Heaven, for the "sure word" of Thy Prophets and Apostles who spake, as commanded, the word for the healing of the nations. Help us to familiarize ourselves with Thy truth. May we never be ashamed of it, but defend it now that it may defend us both here and hereafter. We ask for Jesus' sake. Amen.

ELABORATION.

Our need—the utility of the canon of Scripture—its scope, purpose, power, promises, privileges. Search as testimony of Jesus and eternal life. Search earnestly, regularly, carefully, humbly, methodically. It is a library. The *rich* word of testimony, wisdom, victory, prophecy and success. Note: It illumines, quickens, cleanses and emancipates. It is a hammer, a two-edged sword, a mirror, the soul's food.

APPLICATION.

Use the Gospel, God's power unto salvation, the soul's shield; use as an arsenal for the soul-winner. See example of Jesus in temptation. In teaching, with two disciples on the way to Emmaus. Understand difference between the old and the new Gospel committed to the Apostles.

Am I blessed in keeping the word of the Lord? Do I rejoice therein? Am I ready with the soft answer to turn away wrath and to give a reason for my faith? Do I resist temptation by the power of God's word within? Can I win souls by being expert with the sword of the Spirit?

Don't be afraid of " Higher Criticism " or the study of " Comparative Religions." The World's Parliament of Religions demonstrated the superiority of

Christianity and the Christian Scriptures over all forms and expressions of faith.

LESSON IX. OUTLINED.
KNOWLEDGE OF MANKIND.

DEVOTION.

O our Father, may we understand the words of our blessed Lord, "Inasmuch as thou didst it unto one of the least of these, thou didst it unto me." Help us to see Thy image in humanity, though marred and effaced. With Thy power may we take the yielding stone and place thereon Thy image yet again. For Jesus' sake.

ELABORATION.

Consider the possibilities of a man in Jesus Christ, shown in trial, physical, intellectual and spiritual.

" 'So near is glory to our dust—so near is
            God to man,
  When duty whispers low 'Thou must,' the
            Youth replies, 'I can.' ' "

The test comes in sowing and not reaping, in doing right without reward, in cutting off kindred for truth's sake.

Consanguineous Ties.—If one member of the household is joined to Christ and His people, ordinarily that member, be it boy or girl, wife or husband, is the one who can exercise most influence upon the other members of the family. Be not diffident or procrastinating about exercising such influence. If you can save them, do so; but if there be such an emergency that you must either give up your faith and obedience in Christ, in a word, your soul's integrity, or your people, your duty is clear.

Note, if the soul be unconverted it is "dead in sin," "condemned," "miserable," "blind," "naked," "mad," "an enemy," "hopeless," "deaf," "without excuse," "lost!" But if converted, the antithesis, *i. e.*, "alive," "without condemnation," "happy," "can hear," "justified," "forgiven," "saved!"

APPLICATION.

"Because others failed, not you, therefore. We live not by what we are, but by what we long to be. No one finds a place, but makes a place. We find opportunities to some extent; it is love that nerves us with incessant affirmations. The moment we admit the carping, fretful, uncharitable words, then we disintegrate our force."

The motor for all right achievement lies in an atmosphere of righteousness and peace and joy of the Holy Ghost. Your object in knowing man is that there may be an abundant entrance into His Kingdom.

LESSON X. OUTLINED.

What Sin Is.

DEVOTION.

Deliver us, O deliver us by Thy strength in the inner man from the committal and consequences of sin—that subtle, deceitful and deadly foe that haunts our every

thought and act. O we thank Thee for
the victory through Jesus Christ our
Lord. Washed in the blood of the Lamb,
made clean every whit! Blessed be Thy
wondrous health, forever and forever,
world without end. Amen.

ELABORATION.

Sin defined, "Transgression of law,"
1 John 3: 4; "Transgression through
ignorance," Rom. 10: 3; "Omission of
duty," Jas. 4: 17; Every one a sinner,
1 John 1: 8; 1 John 5: 19; Gal. 9: 22;
Devil the author, 1 John 3: 8 and
John 8: 44; Comes from the heart,
Matt. 15: 19; Mark 7; 21-23.

Sin is (a) Rebellion against God.
Titus 1: 16. (b) Abominable to God.
Prov. 15: 9. God knows them all.
Psalms 69: 5; Psalms 90: 8. Sin is the
fruit of lust. Jas. 1: 15, and the sting of
death. 1 Cor. 15: 56. *Unbelievers* " excuse," "love," "meditate upon," "are
servants of," "throw blame on others,"
"deny their own," "tempt others to sin
and are dead in sin." Sin leads to re-

morse, shame, afflictions, death. Where-
ever sin is made light of, palliated and
condoned, beware! This is a truly deadly
heresy.

APPLICATION.

Believers should depart from all sin,
avoid the appearance of, be watchful
against, strive against, not partake of
others, reprove and rebuke. By God's
grace this is the sum of our work—to save
and be saved from sin. Those who trust
and obey Jesus, are ashamed of past sins,
shall be forgiven and freed from the
guilt and power of sin. Sin is sin, and
one sin of whatever character has in it
all sin, as the seed has in it the tree.

SIN.

Lord, with what care hast thou begirt us round!
   Parents first season us; then schoolmasters
Deliver us to laws; they send us bound
   To rules of reason, holy messengers:

Pulpits and Sundays; sorrow dogging sin;
   Afflictions sorted, anguish of all sizes;
Fine nets and stratagems to catch us in;
   Bibles laid open; millions of surprises;

Blessings beforehand ; ties of gratefulness ;
  The sound of glory in our ears ;
Without, our shame; within, our consciences;
  Angels and grace ; eternal hopes and fears,
Yet all these fences, and their whole array,
  One cunning bosom-sin blows quite away.
                 —*George Herbert.*

LESSON XI. OUTLINED.
KNOW DOCTRINES.

DEVOTION.

O our Father, purge our rubbish-filled minds, give only Thy teachings and truth. May we understand that in Thy kingdom our functions are neither legislative nor judicial. May we understand the precepts and example of our blessed Lord. We ask for his sake. Amen.

ELABORATION.

The true and only apostolic succession of our day is to be accounted faithful and capable of imparting the doctrines of Jesus Christ. Caution.—"For when for the time ye ought to be teachers, ye
  7

have need that one teach you again the
first principles of the oracles of God."
Not confounding the "faith which was
once for all delivered unto the saints"
with the conflicting notions of men, which
are as varied as the customs of men and
as the procession of the centuries.

"If any man teach a different doctrine
and consent not to sound words—the
words of our Lord Jesus Christ, and to
the doctrine which is according to godliness—he is puffed up, knowing nothing
but doting about questionings and dis-
putes of words," (thus the clashing
creeds of men,) "whereof cometh envy,
strife, railings, evil surmisings, wran-
glings of men, corrupted in mind and be-
reft of truth, supposing that godliness is
a way of gain."

It is said that this matter of doctrine is
a question of interpretation, and every
man has a right to his own interpretation.

Concerning Interpretation, notice—
Helps. (a) Common sense; (b) Mental industry; (c) Honest heart; (d) As
general and thorough an education as

possible. *Hindrances.* (a) Desire to please the world; (b) The Bible the property of a select few; (c) Used to prove pet doctrines; (d) Bible a book of wonders only; (e) Not intended to understand; (f) Thirst for distinction.

Consider the following methods or kinds of interpretation:

I. Mystic Method—from Greek *meao,* "to shut the eyes." (a) Originated in mythology and heathendom; (b) Adopted by an apostate church to make priests respected. *Objections.* (a) Permits and fosters superstition and sects; (b) If the Bible does not mean what it says, how can we know what it does mean?

II. Hierarchical Method—by priests. (a) Makes the church the interpreter of the Bible; (b) Takes the Bible away from the common people.

III. Rationalistic Method—that we have reason and no need of revelation. (a) Irrational use of reason; (b) All new truth at first appears unreasonable; (c) This method takes no account of internal and historical evidences and testimonies.

I V. Dogmatic Method—(a) Rests upon scholasticism, *i. e.*, trained men for
defense of doctrine; (b) a searching for
special doctrine—"Trinity," "Transub-
stantiation," "Total Hereditary Depravity," etc.; (c) exalts tradition and specu-
lations of men to a level with God's word.

V. Inductive Method, "in ductio"—
(a) Supposed freedom from bias; (b)
goes from particular to general; (c) the
sum of observations and experiences; (d)
Law, History, Medicine, this method; (e)
bad tendency to deduce before we sufficiently induce; (f) uses analysis and synthesis; (g) this method more than eclec-
tic — *ab initio* different — as difference
between a God revealed and an idol manufactured.

APPLICATION.

2 Tim. 2: 22-25: "But flee youthful
lusts, and follow after righteousness,
faith, love, peace, with them that call
on the Lord out of a pure heart. But
foolish and ignorant questionings refuse,
knowing that they gender strifes. And

the Lord's servant must not strive, but be gentle towards all, apt to teach, forbearing, in meekness correcting them that oppose themselves. If peradventure God · may give them repentance unto the knowledge of the truth."

John 7: 16, 17: "Jesus therefore answered them, and said, My teaching is not mine, but his that sent me. If any man willeth to do his will, he shall know of the teaching, whether it be of God, or whether I speak from myself."

LESSON XII. OUTLINED.

JUDGMENT.

DEVOTION.

We praise Thee, O Lord, that Thou art known by the judgment Thou executest. Established in Thy righteousness, may we ever confess it just. Help us that we may understand Thy decrees and be content with Thy sovereign Judgeship. We ask for Jesus' sake. Amen.

ELABORATION.

God's judgment is (1) without respect of persons; (2) according to deeds; (3) according to words; (4) according to the thoughts; (5) according to the use of entrusted gifts and talents; (6) the words spoken by Christ shall judge men. John 12: 48: "Take heed therefore how ye hear."

Man's judgment. (1) Judge not; (2) reflex—as ye judge so shall ye be judged: (3) by external appearances; (4) always with lack of data—must determine his own action—*i. e.,* "Let every man be fully persuaded in his own mind."

APPLICATION.

We too often arrogate to ourselves the prerogative of the Almighty, hence, church strife. Withholding judgment does not necessarily involve surrender, or even compromise principle. "One is our Master." Engross this motto on the tablet of your heart and bigotry and conceit and vanity and pride will withdraw.

In treating with those out of Christ, we

reason with them and do not judge them; we present Christ to them; they stand condemned by their own action if Christ is rejected. Take pains and present the true Christ!

LESSON XIII. OUTLINED.

PRINCIPLES OF IMPARTING FAITH.

DEVOTION.

We thank Thee for the abundant facilities of our day for teaching Thy truth. Grant to us a breadth and depth of principle that shall accomplish Thy will among men. For Jesus' sake.

ELABORATION.

Man is infinitely honored in being made the dwelling-place, custodian and medium of divine life. "That which is born of the flesh is flesh, and that which is born of the Spirit is spirit."

Principle: (1) *Point of sympathy*— Adapt what is said and done to win the soul to that soul's condition and capacity to grasp.

(2) *Take the soul with you*—Maintain the attention and co-operative industry of the soul in its apprehension of, and obedience to, divine truth.

(3) *Use of illustrations* — Familiar, easy to be understood; for both eye and ear; the child needs more than the adult.

(4) *Necessity of repetition*—So little is retained; it must be blow after blow; the familiar is enjoyed because it means thoroughness; give the outline of prayer again and again and again; the same moral precepts viewed again and again from all angles.

APPLICATION.

By and by you marshal all these apt and saving truths that have been driven by blow after blow into the very life of the soul, and the soul can withstand the demands of the faith no longer, but yields a loving obedience to the Christ, "is buried with him by baptism unto death " to rise in the new life of the blessed Holy Spirit, whereof its tunefulness and fragrance shall make all earth and heaven rejoice.

PART III.

THE KINGDOM OF GOD.

LESSON I. OUTLINED.

THE KINGDOM AS OUTLINED BY JESUS CHRIST IN THE GOSPELS.

DEVOTION.

We thank Thee, O our Heavenly Father, for the glorious vision of the New Jerusalem—the white four-square city, where the power of Thy Spirit, felt, though unseen, extends over all its beneficent sway. May we expect, desire and labor for none other than that kingdom inaugurated and described by Jesus the Lord!

ELABORATION.

The Kingdom obscured because thought of as some scholastic ecclesiasticism. Not so. John heralded the coming King and kingdom—the Christ and His Spirit reign. Jesus sets forth in His beatitudes (Matt. 5: 3-16 and the like) the character of its subjects, and describes the Kingdom in the many parables: "It is like" (1) Sower; (2) Leaven; (3) Treasure in

Field; (4) Mustard Seed; (5) Net Cast into the Sea; (6) Marriage of the King's Son; (7) Ten Virgins; (8) The Talents, etc.; and is further described in other figures as Christ's Household, sheep-fold, etc.

Kingdom and Church synonymously used: The word "Church" occurs but twice in the Gospels. Matt. 16:18, "And I also say unto thee, that thou art Peter, and upon this rock I will build my Church; and the gates of Hades shall not prevail against it." Matt. 18:17, "And if he refuse to hear them, tell it unto the Church: and if he refuse to hear the Church also, let him be unto thee as the Gentile and the publican." The word used here as "church," and elsewhere as "kingdom," means "assembled," "associated," "realm" and cognate expressions to cover the various ideas of ruler and subjects, institutes and ordinances, also the Gospel dispensation—the extension and general diffusion of the Christianity of Christ.

THE SURE FOUNDATION STONE.

The foolish builders, scribe and priest,
 Reject it with disdain;
Yet on this rock the Church shall rest,
 And envy rage in vain.

What though the gates of Hell withstood,
 Yet must this building rise:
'Tis thine own work, Almighty God,
 And wondrous in our eyes.

—Isaac Watts.

APPLICATION.

The Kingdom is not, (1) a club of speculators in either physics or metaphysics; (2) the piously disposed followers of fashion; (3) an association of æsthetic literary characters; (4) an aggregation of self-satisfied religious devotees. The Kingdom occupies ground infinitely higher and broader and deeper than any one or all of these. It is of Divine origin, with appointments adapted to bring the entire family of man into harmony with the will of God, and we are fellow-laborers with God. Where do I stand?

LESSON II. OUTLINED.

THE FIRST CHRISTIAN CHURCH, AND HOW
THE APOSTLES MADE DISCIPLES.

DEVOTION.

We adore Thee, O Thou infinitely loving One, for all the provisions for and
associations of grace. May we faithfully
follow Him who is the author and finisher
of our faith until His blessed brother-
hood girdles the globe. Amen.

ELABORATION.

The Acts of the Apostles is an exceed-
ingly important book, especially in this
connection, as it is the authentic and accurate history that every soul-winner must
know in order to build upon the sure
foundation.

Read the first and second chapters, and
especially Acts 2: 41, 42, for the nature
and essential conditions of church fellowship and communion: (1) Baptism, im-
plying faith and repentance; (2) Apostolic doctrine and teaching; (3) The
Lord's Supper; (4) Public worship—thus

enumerated and established for all time. Beginning at Jerusalem the Word was to go forth (Luke 24: 47). Notice how disciples were made (first) on the day of Pentecost: (a) Holy Ghost (Acts 2: 33; 1: 4, 5, 8; 2: 4); (b) Peter's work, the speaker (Acts 2: 14, 37); Kingdom to be set up (Matt. 16: 18; Acts 1: 6-8; Dan. 2: 44; Matt. 3: 2; 4: 17; 10: 7; Luke 10: 9).

Conditions of citizenship stated (Acts 2: 38, 41, 47). Argument in detail as to induce faith (Acts 2: 14-36). The people's work (Acts 2: 37, 41, 42, 47). The kingdom begins as spoken and promised in Daniel and Luke 24: 17. Baptized "into His name," *i. e.,* in submission to his authority. Continuing the history in Acts, see also case of the Samaritan, Acts 8: 1-17; eunuch, Acts 8: 25-40; Saul, Acts 9: 1-18; 22: 6-16; first Gentiles, Acts 10: 30-48; Lydia and household, Acts 16: 13-15; Philippian jailer, Acts 16: 25-34; general statements, Acts 11: 20, 21; 18: 8, and Romans 10: 11-17.

Miracles in the Early Church.—Purpose (Acts 14: 3; 19: 11, 12, and 1 Cor. 14: 22). Truth once established miracles cease (1 John 5: 9, 10; Luke 16: 29-31; 1 Cor. 12: 30, 31, and 1 Cor. 13). Why, then, have miracles (in that sense) ceased? Answer: The purpose is accomplished; what began in miracle continues by natural law, *i. e.*, ordained agencies; thus the facts of creation. See Gen. 1: 11, 28. In a miraculous way the church is originated; the "Gospel" is its means of reproduction.

Notice Paul's illustration of the Kingdom and its Unity (Eph. 4: 1-16):

(a) Unity of Headship—"One Lord."

(b) Unity of belief—"One Faith."

(c) Unity of obedience—"One Baptism."

(d) Unity of hope of eternal life—"One hope of your calling."

(e) Unity of "Spirit in bond of peace."

(f) Unity of organization — "One Body."

APPLICATION.

Beware the tendency toward intolerance, narrowness, and toward giving local coloring and boundaries to the Church, destroying thus its beauty, power and universality.

Notice.—We are set for the restoration of the faith—its fruits, its ordinances and its life—for the Kingdom in its fullness. How do you stand this moment?

GLORIOUS ZION.

Glorious things of thee are spoken,
Zion, city of our God!
He whose word cannot be broken,
Formed thee for His own abode.
On the Rock of Ages founded,
What can shake thy sure repose!
>—*John Newton.*

LESSON III. OUTLINED.

ORGANIZATION.

DEVOTION.

We love Thy Kingdom, O Lord. Grant that we may not dread the drudgery of detailed duty. We pray Thee that the

8

agencies and machinery for the evangelization of the great cities and of the world may be forthcoming, and that this soul-winners' training-class may contribute to this glorious end. To Thee we will ascribe all praise, through Jesus Christ our Lord. Amen.

ELABORATION.

The constitutional principle in the life of the Kingdom is *Love* (John 13: 34, 35; 1 John 4: 7, 8; 1 Tim. 1: 5-7; 1 Cor. 13). Hence the true purpose and scope of discipline and edification is to build up and preserve in Love.

Organization means to give instruments or organs of action. Is there a work to do? There must be an order of procedure—a way to do it—"first apostles, then evangelists, pastors, teachers." The work and its character called for the workers and determined their character and duties (Acts 6: 3-5). Consider the nature of the work of the Kingdom. Is it legislative? No; Christ gave the constitutional law, and established the nature of

its precepts and institutes forever. Is it
judicial? No, certainly not primarily so;
God is sole Judge. The fruits make manifest—our lives too short and eyes too
dim to see all fruit. The final day shall
reveal all. Christ's word shall judge.
What, then, is the character of the work?
It is *administrative*—"oversee," "feed,"
"serve." Beginning with Love, Faith
and Hope must follow. We have worked
from the wrong end. Mark this, it is
vital and fundamental. Don't think to
work through Faith and Hope to attain
Love, but to work through Love to attain
Faith and Hope. *Christ-like* service is
the secret.

"It is said truly that hundreds of ingenious inventions die every year for lack of
ready hands to seize upon and work them,
while hundreds more die because, while
they have been in the course of development, other and better ones have super-
seded them." The Church has been en-
deavoring for more than eighteen centuries to apply the gospel to humanity:
most ingenious have been many of the

plans and methods. Nature is full of organization, and the patent-office is full of
inventions; and man, as he attains purposes spiritual, seeks an orderly arrange-
ment for the expression and execution of
such purposes. But organizations within
the Church have multiplied. Certainly.
We organize for this, that and the other
thing, and everything. Of course; and
just as our thought and purposes intens-
ify and widen, we will continue. But organizations are defective; yes, and so are
purposes. Now at any given time the
thing containing the highest, best developed and truest purpose will arrive at the
corresponding least defective organization; they are so essentially correlated.
Witness foreign missions. Burden the
Church with the sincere purpose to con-
vert the heathen, and it finds practical
issue through organization. As the purpose grows and is purified and intensified,
the organization seeks to adjust itself to
reduce friction and facilitate a practical
co-operation conformable to the law of
economy.

· All too defective are our organizations, as all too lame and halt are our purposes. The battle is by no means won—barely begun; let us hold the vantage ground and press on.

APPLICATION.

Take home to yourself the reasonableness of the foregoing view, because it is set forth in the Scriptures and is conceded by the Christian world; in it is the requisite latitude for diversity of talents coexistent with the complexities of the field, the true unity in diversity.

ROOM FOR YOU.

Who shall sweep away the errors
    Crowding on us from the past?
Who shall clear the mists and shadows
    That the future overcast?

Soon we busy, teeming millions,
    Will have ended all this strife ;
And the myriads crowding on us
    Must take up the task of life.

Ah! the workers in the vineyard
    Are too faint and all to few ;
And the field of honest effort
    Ever waits, young friends, for you.

Room for boyhood, strong and sturdy—
　Boyhood manly, brave and true;
Room for honest, lusty vigor—
　Room, my young friends—room for you.

Room for every sweet-voiced singer
　That can thrill the heart with song;
Room for thoughts, and words, and actions,
　That will drive the world along.
　　　　　　—*George R. Howarth.*

LESSON V. OUTLINED.

The Visible and Local Congregation.

DEVOTION.

O our Divine Father, accept our praise for Thy wondrous economy. Grant that we may apprehend the things divinely practical to the end that now and here Thy will may be done and Thy Kingdom come in fullness. We ask for Jesus' sake.

ELABORATION.

The idea of the Church invisible and universal comes from that of the visible and local, else intangible and impracticable, and as a matter of fact this statement stands unimpeached. The officers we read of in the New Testament are almost entirely for service in the local congrega-'tion. The desirability and necessity for co-operation among local congregations gave rise to officers with various functions; all such retained fellowship in some local congregation. The ordinances —baptism and the Lord's Supper—are not to be conceived as having an invisible, universal existence, but on the contrary are dependent upon local congregations for their perpetuity.

One is culpable if being engrossed in the work of the local congregation he is disloyal to the general co-operation, and vice versa, viz., being so engrossed in the ultra-spiritualized work of the general movement as to be out of harmony with the local congregation. No man can belong to an army unless he belongs to a company.

Christians "in the broad," *i. e.*, not affiliated with a congregation, are not in Christ's fold, but trying some other way.

Christ ordained the local, as also the general, but the latter through the former.

APPLICATION.

Many we visit are singularly ethereal Christians. Yes, "Christians," but not enlisted for duty; soldiers on a strictly "peace-footing." What an anomaly. How is it with yourself?

LESSON V. OUTLINED.

THINGS DONE TO BUILD UP THE CONGREGATION.

DEVOTION.

O our Father, we thank Thee for the glorious participation in Thy Cause and Kingdom. May we exercise ourselves to the salvation of ourselves and those whom we may be instrumental in influencing, acknowledging and using all the blessed means of Grace vouchsafed to us through Jesus Christ our Lord, to whom be glory and majesty, dominion and power, henceforth and evermore. Amen.

ELABORATION.

The object of Law is the preservation of life. "An ordinance (law) is a rule established by authority."—*Webster*. The ordinances are, (1) "Baptism;" (2) Lord's Supper;" (3) "Prayer;" (4) "Blessing" or "Praise and Thanksgiving;" (5) "Teaching;" (6) "Serving;" (7) "Giving;" (8) "Showing mercy;" (9) "Presiding." Participation of the members in public worship is for edification. Read 1 Cor. 14: 26, 33, 40.

APPLICATION.

The Sunday-school, Young People's Societies, Church Extension Boards, etc., with the classes in soul-winning, serve some, many, or all of these ordinances, as the case may be; therefore an integral part of the Church as a unit, and if conducted in the spirit of their formation are growths, not outside of, distinct from, or in any way antagonistic to, the church, local or general; but on the contrary are parts of an harmonious whole, manifesting the varied activities of that present organization which is destined, under its divine Founder and Leader to conquer the world!

LESSON VI. OUTLINED.

RELATION OF CONGREGATIONS TO EACH OTHER.

DEVOTION.

Especially are we grateful, O Lord, for the fellowship of the saints that broadens our service and our sympathy. Help us in our acts of co-operation and missionary enterprises till Thy Kingdom come in the hearts of all in blessed fullness.

ELABORATION.

I. Older churches planted new ones and provided for their instruction: (a) Jerusalem Church, Acts 8: 14-17, 25, 40; Acts 9: 31, 32; Acts 11: 19-26; (b) Antioch Church, Acts 13: 1-5; Acts 14: 23-28; Acts 15: 40; 1 Thes. 2: 5-16; Gal. 2: 9.

II. By means of *Committees* or delegates, congregations conferred on matters of teaching and discipline, Acts 15: 1-6.

III. Congregations co-operated by means of Committees in relieving distress in time of famine, Acts 11: 27-30; Acts 12: 25; 1 Cor. 16: 1-4; 2 Cor. 8: 1-15; 2 Cor. 9: 1-5. So carry the Bread of Life to all—no foreign country—all earth is unalienized.

IV. Co-operated in supporting evangelist in starting new work, 2 Cor. 11: 8-9; 1 Tim. 5: 17-19; Phil. 4: 14-18; 1 Cor. 16: 15-18.

V. Co-operation avoids waste, overlapping, the prejudice of ignorance, while it fosters and induces economy, promotes acquaintance and wisdom, develops power, concentrates endeavor and fulfills the will and purpose of God in Christ. In our day if Protestants and Roman Catholics were one in Christ, how it would exalt the Book, the Christ and heavenly love!

How it would dismay and dumbfound the devil! How it would spread the earth as the waters of the deep and no man could say, "No one careth for my soul."

If as one man we could unite in conducting charities, in enforcing law and order, suppressing impure literature, and in the promotion of temperance to the absolute prohibition of the poisonous alcoholic beverages, how quickly the jails, workhouses and penitentiaries, the hospitals and the eleemosynary institutions would disappear! Instead of influencing and saving a possible one-fifth of our youth and one-fifth of our adult population, to have our youth and adult citizenship, knowing neither male nor female, not only nominally, but really Christians, O how it . would relegate to the limbo of darkness and death from whence they spring, the unscrupulous competitions and awful enorities of so-called respectable businesses that now mar and blight all branches of civil and religious life! Why so sure of this? Because disciples cannot be united until we become "one as I am in the Father." This, the sublime, harmonious symphony of earth and heaven.

PART IV.

DISOBEDIENCE EXAMINED.

INTRODUCTION.

While the excuses for declining to obey Christ are almost innumerable, nevertheless arrows of truth in the Bible quiver are plentiful to pierce them all.

We come now to the "face-to-face" work, when soul wrestles with soul. Only those who have been so engaged may know the soul-winner's unspeakable pleasure in seeing the lip quiver, the eye suffuse with tears and the bosom swell with intense emotion as the soul is brought into the Kingdom; and as for such soul in its obedience,

> "Earth has a joy unknown in heaven,
> The new-born joy of sins forgiven!
> Tears of such pure and deep delight,
> O angels, never dimmed your sight."

O soul-winner, work in no other spirit than God's Holy Spirit! Converse with one person at a time and out of hearing of others if possible. Seek for seriousness; proceed cautiously; find by judicious questioning the state of the one out of Christ—to what class he belongs and what his condition, difficulties, reasons, excuses and objections are; then fix your mind on his individuality. All the work of Jesus Christ, the prophets and apostles, all your studies in soul-winning are to fit you for this occasion. Put into it all your intellectual and spiritual vigor. (Necessarily from the abridged character of this treatise, all shades of disobedience cannot be discussed, only outlines are attempted.) Seek for the point of sympathy and insert the Gospel blade, "For the word of God is quick," etc. Heb. 4: 13.

SECTION A.

THE SUPERFICIAL.

A vast number belong to this class, and so mixed, complicated and conflicting are the conditions that we must overcome indifference and superficiality by our earnestness and insight; although a difficulty appears shallow and slight to you, it may be real and serious to the halting one.

All classes enter into the blessings and benedictions of Christianity, although many neither confess Christ nor support His cause. Such stupidity and ingratitude would be incredible if it were not so common and so patent.

I. LACK OF DEEP CONVICTION.

Matt. 13: 5, 6: "And others fell upon the rocky places, where they had not much earth: and straightway they sprang up, because they had no deepness of earth: and when the sun was risen, they were scorched; and because they had no root they withered away."

John 1: 10: "He was in the world, and the world was made by him, and the world knew him not."

Matt. 22: 5: "But they made light of it, and went their ways, one to his own farm, another to his merchandise."

II. "STILL A LITTLE SKEPTICAL."

John 7: 16, 17: "Jesus therefore answered them, and said, My teaching is not

9

mine, but his that sent me. If any man
willeth to do his will, he shall know of
the teaching, whether it be of God, or
whether I speak from myself."

John 20: 31: "But these are written
that ye may believe that Jesus is the
Christ, the Son of God; and that believ-
ing, ye may have life in his name."

III.   " WAIT UNTIL A MORE CONVENIENT
TIME."

2 Cor. 6: 1, 2: "And working together
with him we entreat also that ye receive
not the grace of God in vain. (For he
saith, At an acceptable time I hearkened
unto thee, And in a day of salvation did I
succour thee; behold, now is the acceptable time; behold, now is the day of salvation)."

Heb. 3: 13: " But exhort one another
day by day, so long as it is called to-day;
lest any one of you be hardened by the
deceitfulness of sin."

Acts 24: 25: "And as he reasoned of
righteousness, and temperance, and the
judgment to come, Felix was terrified,

and answered, Go thy way for this time; and when I have a convenient season, I will call thee unto me."

Jas. 4: 13, 14: "Go to now, ye that say, To-day or to-morrow we will go into this city, and spend a year there, and trade and get gain; whereas ye know not what shall be on the morrow. What is your life? For ye are a vapour, that appeareth for a little time, and then vanisheth away."

Jas. 4: 17: "To him therefore that knoweth to do good, and doeth it not, to him it is sin."

Eccl. 12: 1: "Remember also thy Creator in the days of thy youth, or ever the evil days come, and the years draw nigh, when thou shalt say, I have no pleasure in them."

Prov. 8: 17: "I love them that love me; and those that seek me diligently shall find me."

Isa. 55: 6: "Seek ye the Lord while he may be found, call ye upon him while he is near."

Matt. 24: 44: "Therefore be ye also

ready: for in an hour that ye think not the Son of man cometh.''

Heb. 3: 15: '' While it is said, To-day if ye shall hear his voice, harden not your hearts, as in the provocation.''

IV. LOVE OF EASE.

Matt. 10: 38, 39: ''And he that doth not take his cross and follow after me, is not worthy of me. He that findeth his life shall lose it; and he that loseth his life for my sake shall find it.''

Matt. 19: 27, 29: '' Then answered Peter and said unto him, Lo, we have left all, and followed thee; what then shall we have? And every one that hath left houses, or brethren, or sisters, or father, or mother, or children or lands, for my name's sake, shall receive a hundred fold, and shall inherit eternal life.''

V. NOT CALLED YET—WANT SPECIAL SIGN.

Acts 22: 16: ''And now why tarriest thou? Arise, and be baptized, and wash away thy sins, calling on His name.''

Luke 19: 41, 42: ''And when he drew

nigh, he saw the city, and wept over it, saying, If thou hadst known in this day, even thou, the things which belong unto peace! but now they are hid from thine eyes."

Matt. 12: 38, 39: "Then certain of the scribes and Pharisees answered him, saying, Master, we would see a sign from thee. But he answered and said unto them, An evil and adulterous generation seeketh after a sign: and there shall no sign be given to it but the sign of Jonah the prophet."

Luke 16: 30, 31: "And he said, Nay, father Abraham: but if one go to them from the dead, they will repent. And he said unto him, If they hear not Moses and the prophets, neither will they be persuaded, if one rise from the dead."

Rom. 1: 16: "For I am not ashamed of the gospel: for it is the power of God unto salvation to every one that believeth; to the Jew first and also to the Greek."

VI.   CONTROVERSIAL SPIRIT.

Matt. 22: 15, 23, 34, 35, 41, 42: "Then went the Pharisees, and took counsel how they might ensnare him in his talk. On that day there came to him Sadducees, which say that there is no resurrection. But the Pharisees, when they heard that he had put the Sadducees to silence, gathered themselves together. And one of them, a lawyer, asked him a question, tempting him. Now while the Pharisees were gathered together, Jesus asked them a question, saying, What think ye of the Christ? whose Son is he? They say unto him, The son of David."

VII.   "WONT BELIEVE WHAT I DO NOT UNDERSTAND."

John 3: 9: "Nicodemus answered and said unto him, How can these things be?"

John 6: 52: "The Jews therefore strove with one another, saying, How can this man give us his flesh to eat?"

John 6: 60: "Many therefore of his disciples, when they heard this, said, This is a hard saying; who can hear it?"

Acts 17: 32: "Now when they heard of the resurrection of the dead, some mocked; but others said, We will hear thee concerning this yet again."

1 Cor. 2: 14: "Now the natural man receiveth not the things of the Spirit of God: for they are foolishness unto him; and he cannot know them, because they are spiritually examined."

2 Cor. 8: 12: "For if the readiness is there, it is acceptable according as a man hath, not according as he hath not."

Rom. 10: 8: "But what saith it? The word is nigh thee, in thy mouth, and in thy heart: that is the word of faith which we preach."

2 Peter 3: 16: "As also in all his epistles, speaking in them of these things; wherein are some things hard to be understood, which the ignorant and unstedfast wrest, as they do also the other scriptures, unto their own destruction."

PRAYER.

O our Father in heaven, help us as we engage in thy blessed work. May we have a ready mind and plain speech to convince the wavering and move them to action; and grant that our work may stand the tests of time· and eternity. We ask for Jesus' sake. Amen.

SECTION .B.

THE APOSTATE.

There are those open apostates who go "out from us, because they are not of us." There are those reprobates who are still maintaining some sort of a profession of religion, but lead wicked lives. There are also those who with their religious pretensions maintain a fair outward life, but are backsliders in heart. It is a most sad and unsettled condition—most unaccountable excuses and flimsy difficulties are presented. Great forbearance and patience are required to work with such characters, because one feels that as they fell away once, they perhaps are subject to falls. Remember God's grace is sufficient for us and for them.

VIII. (1) "CANNOT HOLD OUT."

Jer. 2: 13: "For my people have committed two evils; they have forsaken me, the fountain of living waters, and hewed them out cisterns, that can hold no water."

1 Cor. 10: 13: "There hath no temptation taken you but such as man can bear: but God is faithful, who will not suffer you to be tempted above that ye are able; but will with the temptation make also the way of escape, that ye may be able to endure it."

Rom. 8: 38, 39: "For I am persuaded, that neither death, nor life, nor angels, nor principalities, nor things present, nor things to come, nor powers, nor height, nor depth, nor any other creature, shall be able to separate us from the love of God, which is in Christ Jesus our Lord."

Mark 4: 18, 19: "And others are they that are sown among the thorns; these are they that have heard the word, and the cares of the world, and the deceitfulness of riches, and the lusts of other things entering in, choke the word, and it becometh unfruitful."

John 10: 27-30: "My sheep hear my voice, and I know them, and they follow me: And I give unto them eternal life; and they shall never perish, and no one shall snatch them out of my hand. My Father, which hath given them unto me, is greater than all; and no one is able to snatch them out of the Father's hand. I and the Father are one."

Rev. 3: 14-17: "And to the angel of the church in Laodicea write: These things saith the Amen, the faithful and true witness, the beginning of the creation of God: I know thy works, that thou art neither cold nor hot: I would thou were cold or hot. So because thou art lukewarm, and neither hot nor cold, I will spew thee out of my mouth."

IX. (2) "TRIED WITHOUT SUCCESS."

John 8: 12: "Again therefore Jesus spake unto them, saying, I am the light of the world: he that followeth me shall not walk in the darkness, but shall have the light of life."

1 Peter 4: 19: "Wherefore let them also that suffer according to the will of God, commit their souls in well-doing unto a faithful Creator."

Prov. 14: 14: "The backslider in heart shall be filled with his own ways; and a good man shall be satisfied from himself."

2 Peter 2: 20, 21: "For if, after they have escaped the defilements of the world through the knowledge of the Lord and Savior Jesus Christ, they are again entangled therein and overcome, the last state is become worse with them than the first. For it were better for them not to have known the way of righteousness, than, after knowing it, to turn back from the holy commandment delivered unto them."

Luke 9: 62: "But Jesus said unto him, No man, having put his hand to the plough, and looking back, is fit for the kingdom of God."

x. (3) "INCONSISTENCIES OF CHRISTIANS."

Jude 12, 13: "These are they who are hidden rocks in your love-feasts when they feast with you, shepherds that without fear feed themselves; clouds without water, carried along by winds; autumn trees without fruit, twice dead, plucked up by the roots; wild waves of the sea, foaming out their own shame; wandering stars, for whom the blackness of darkness hath been reserved forever."

Rom. 14: 4: "Who art thou that judgest the servant of another? to his own lord he standeth or falleth. Yea, he shall be made to stand; for the Lord hath power to make him stand."

Rom. 14: 12: "So then each one of us shall give account of himself to God."

1 John 3: 10: "In this the children of God are manifest, and the children of the devil: whosoever doeth not righteousness is not of God, neither he that loveth not his brother."

John 21: 21, 22: "Peter therefore see-

ing him, saith to Jesus, Lord, and what
shall this man do?   Jesus saith unto him,
If I will that he tarry till I come, what is
that to thee? follow thou me."

XI. (4) "TOO GREAT A SINNER."

Phil. 1: 6: "That the fellowship of thy
faith may become effectual, in the knowledge of every good thing which is in you,
unto Christ."

John 6: 37: "All that which the Father
giveth me shall come unto me; and him
that cometh to me, I will in no wise cast
out."

Isa. 1: 18: "Come, now, and let us
reason together, saith the Lord: though
your sins be as scarlet, they shall be as
white as snow; though they be red like
crimsom, they shall be as wool."

1 Peter 2: 24, 25: "Who his own self
bare our sins in his body upon the tree,
that we, having died unto sins, might live
unto righteousness; by whose stripes ye
were healed.   For ye were going astray
like sheep: but are now returned unto
the Shepherd and Bishop of your soul."

PRAYER.

O our Father, we thank Thee for all Thy blessed promises. Grant that the environment of all may be so surcharged with Christian sentiment that our weaker brethren may find no occasion of stumbling. Forgive the hosts of the backsliding Israel who come back to Thee from wretched wanderings in the wilderness of sin. For Jesus' sake. Amen.

SECTION C.

THE BEWILDERED.

Confusion is the occasion of accidents, calamities and disasters, and which in turn are joined to superstition. It is said, "It is better to have no opinion of God at all, than such an opinion as is unworthy of Him; for the one is unbelief, the other is contumely; and certainly superstition is the reproach of Deity." However, of two such ills, little practical purpose is served by determining (if we were able) which is the greater. Igno-

rance and false lights entail enslaving
enormities upon the sons of men, and if
there be added thereto extreme reverence
for tradition, progress would be effectually blocked. The very best of us are
only partially enlightened; each year and
day adds its quota of light, if so be we
are ever moving towards that goal in
which there is fullness of light.

XII. (1) THE SUPERSTITIOUS.

Matt. 24: 24, 25: "For there shall rise
false Christs, and false prophets, and
shall show great signs and wonders; so as
to lead astray, if possible, even the elect.
Behold, I have told you beforehand."

Acts 17: 22, 23, 25, 29: "And Paul
stood in the midst of the Areopagus, and
said, Ye men of Athens, in all things I
perceive that ye are somewhat superstitious. For as I passed along, and observed the objects of your worship, I
found also an altar with this inscription,
TO AN UNKNOWN GOD. What therefore ye
worship in ignorance, this set I forth unto
you. He dwelleth not in temples made

with hands; neither is he served by men's
hands, as though he needed anything,
seeing he himself giveth to all life, and
breath, and all things; and he made of
one every nation of men to dwell on all
the face of the earth. Being then the
offspring of God, we ought not to think
that the Godhead is like unto gold, or silver, or stone, graven by art and device of
man."

XIII. (2) SPIRITUAL BLINDNESS, IGNORANCE.

Luke 4: 18: "He sent me to proclaim
release to the captives, the recovering of
sight to the blind."

Luke 11: 34: "The lamp of thy body
is thine eye: when thine eye is single, thy
whole body also is full of light; but when
it is evil, thy body is also full of darkness."

1 John 1: 5, 6: "And this is the mes-
sage which we have heard from him, and
announce unto you, that God is light, and
in him is no darkness at all. If we say
that we have fellowship with him, and
walk in darkness, we lie, and do not the
truth."

1 John 2: 4: "He that saith I know him, and keepeth not his commandments, is a liar and the truth is not in him."

2 Peter 3: 8, 9: "But forget not this one thing, beloved, that one day is with the Lord as a thousand years, and a thousand years as one day. The Lord is not slack concerning his promise, as some count slackness; but is long-suffering to you-ward, not wishing that any should perish, but that all should come to repentance."

John 17: 3: "And this is life eternal, that they should know thee, the only true God, and him whom thou didst send, Jesus Christ."

Matt. 16: 16: "And Simon Peter answered and said, Thou art the Christ, the Son of the living God."

XIV. (3) HUMAN TRADITIONS TOO MUCH REGARDED.

Matt. 15: 9: "But in vain do they worship me, teaching as their doctrine the precepts of men."

2 Tim. 4: 2, 3: "Preach the Word; be

10

instant in season, out of season; reprove,
rebuke, exhort, with all long-suffering
and teaching. For the time will come
when they will not endure the sound doctrine, but having itching ears, will heap
to themselves teachers after their own
lusts; and will turn away their ears from
the truth, and turn aside unto fables.''

PRAYER.

O our Father, we thank Thee for the
''Light of the World.'' May ignorance,
and superstition and human vanity no
more hold sway over our hearts; help us
to always do those things which are right
in thy sight, whether or not it meet the
approval of men. We ask for Jesus'
sake. Amen

SECTION D.

COMMENDING THEMSELVES.

The human heart is desperately wicked
and deceitful. No one of the ''works of
the flesh''—''fornication, uncleanness,

lasciviousness, idolatry, sorcery, enmities,
strife, jealousies, wraths, factions, divisions, heresies, envyings, drunkenness and
revelings''—but that not only find devotees, but also those who will bring forth
somewhere something to commend in
each.

Rarely, if ever, is the sin, *per se*, com-
mended; but when the individual is involved, the apology is forthcoming; such
is the depth of human depravity as not
only to commit these things, but to boast
of them. This disposition to commend
our practices leads men to fashion God to
suit themselves—to even manufacture
gods of their appetites, their avarice, or
their ambition.

So common and universal is this tendency that some contend there is no revelation of God, *ab extra*, but that man has
only idealized the creations of his own
imagination.

These self-commending people are especially prone to wrest the Scriptures to
their own destruction. Ignorant of the

righteousness of God, they are zealous in establishing their own righteousness.

Disobedience coming directly or indirectly from this predisposition is observable everywhere; intelligent faith alone is capable of successfully contending with such.

XV. (1) LOVE OF PRAISE.

John 12: 43: "They loved the glory of men more than the glory of God."

John 5: 44: "How can ye believe which receive glory one of another, and the glory that cometh from the only God ye seek not?"

Isa. 55: 8: "For my thoughts are not as your thoughts, neither are your ways my ways, saith the Lord."

Prov. 16: 25: "There is a way which seemeth right unto a man, but the end thereof are the ways of death."

XVI. (2) FEAR OF MAN.

John 7: 12, 13: "And there was much murmuring among the multitudes concerning him; some said, He is a good

man; others said, Not so, but he leadeth
the multitude astray. Howbeit no man
spake openly of him for fear of the
Jews."

John 12: 42: "Nevertheless even of
the rulers many believed on him; but because of the Pharisees they did not confess it, lest they should be put out of the
synagogue."

XVII. (3) NOT WILLING TO LEAVE IMPENI-
TENT ASSOCIATES.

2 Cor. 6: 16-18: "And what agreement
hath a temple of God with idols? For we
are a temple of the living God; even as
God said, I will dwell in them, and walk
in them; and I will be their God, and
they shall be my people. Wherefore
come ye out from among them, and be ye
separate, saith the Lord, and touch no
unclean thing; and I will receive you,
and will be to you a Father, and ye shall
be to me sons and daughters, saith the
Lord Almighty."

Luke 18: 29, 30: "And he said unto
them, Verily I say unto you, there is no

man that hath left house, or wife, or
brethren, or parents, or children, for the
kingdom of God's sake, who shall not receive manifold more in this time, and in
the world to come, eternal life.''

Heb. 11: 24-26: ''By faith Moses, when
he was grown up, refused to be called the
son of Pharaoh's daughter; choosing
rather to be evil entreated with the people of God, than to enjoy the pleasure of
sin for a season; accounting the reproach
of Christ greater riches than the treas-
ures of Egypt.''

1 Cor. 7: 16: ''For how knowest thou,
O wife, whether thou shalt save thy husband? Or how knowest thou, O husband,
whether thou shalt save thy wife?''

XVIII. (4) DON'T LIKE THE MESSENGER.

John 1: 46: ''And Nathanael said unto
him, Can any good thing come out of
Nazareth? And Philip said unto him,
Come and see.''

1 Cor. 1: 21: '' For seeing that in the
wisdom of God the world through its wisdom knew not God, it was God's good

pleasure through the foolishness of the
preaching to save them that believed."

1 Cor. 2: 5: "That your faith should
not stand in the wisdom of men, but in
.the power of God."

XIX. (5) INSINCERITY.

Rom. 9: 19, 20: "Thou wilt say unto
me, Why doth he still find fault? for who
understandeth his will? Nay, but, O man,
who art thou that repliest against God?
Shall the thing formed say to him that
formed it, Why didst thou make me
thus?"

Ezek. 18: 25: "Yet ye say, The way
of the Lord is not equal. Hear now, O
house of Israel; is not my way equal? are
not your ways unequal?"

Matt. 21: 28-31: "But what think ye?
A man had two sons; he came to the first,
and said, Son, go work to-day in the vineyard; and he answered and said, I will
not; but afterward he repented himself,
and went. And he came to the second,
and said likewise; and he answered and
said, I go, sir; and went not. Whither

of the twain did the will of his father?
They say, The first. Jesus saith unto
them, Verily I say unto you, that the
publicans and the harlots go into the
kingdom of God before you."

PRAYER.

O our Father, help thou our unbelief!
May the truth work effectually in us. O
may our efforts to save souls be blessed of
Thee to the end that many may gladly re-
ceive and obey Thy word. We ask for
Jesus' sake. Amen.

SECTION E.

FOES WITHIN AND WITHOUT.

In the minds of many disobedient there
is chaos and confusion, and in their
hearts conflicting emotions and desires.
They have not made, nor even attempted,
any clear analysis of their attitude toward
Christ. The foes of the soul within and
without persist in their determination to
neutralize gospel influences, and prevent

the soul from a committal to any definite
and specific stand. The effort to examine
into these complex conditions can be pro-
ductive of good. Persist, then, in prob-
ing, even if it cause a wince now and
then.

XX. (1) TOO MANY THINGS TO GIVE UP.

Phil. 3: 7, 8: "Howbeit what things
were gain to me, these have I counted
loss for Christ. Yea, verily, and I count
all things to be loss for the excellency of
the knowledge of Christ Jesus my Lord."

Mark 8: 36-38: "For what doth it
profit a man to gain the whole world, and
forfeit his life? For what should a man
give in exchange for his life? For whosoever shall be ashamed of me and of my
words in this adulterous and sinful generation, the Son of man also shall be
ashamed of him, when he cometh in the
glory of his Father with the holy angels."

1 Tim. 4: 8: "And exercise thyself
unto godliness; for bodily exercise is
profitable for a little; but godliness is
profitable for all things, having promise

of the life which now is, and of that which is to come."

XXI. (2) PRIDE OF BIRTH.

Matt. 3: 8, 9: "Bring forth therefore fruit worthy of repentance: and think not to say within yourselves, We have Abraham to our father: for I say unto you, that God is able of these stones to raise up children unto Abraham."

John 8: 33, 34: "They answered unto him, We be Abraham's seed, and have never yet been in bondage to any man: how sayest thou, Ye shall be made free? Jesus answered them, Verily, verily, I say unto you, Every one that committeth sin is the bond-servant of sin."

James 2: 1, 5: "My brethren, hold not the faith of our Lord Jesus Christ, the Lord of glory, with respect of persons. Hearken, my beloved brethren; did not God choose them that are poor as to the world to be rich in faith, and heirs of the kingdom which he promised to them that love him?"

Luke 2: 7: "And she brought forth

her firstborn son; and she wrapped him in swaddling clothes, and laid him in a manger, because there was no room for him in the inn."

XXII. (3) TOO SMART.

Matt. 11: 25: "At that season Jesus answered and said, I thank thee, O Father, Lord of heaven and earth, that thou didst hide these things from the wise and understanding, and didst reveal them unto babes."

John 9: 39-41: "And Jesus said, For judgment came I into this world, that they which see not, may see; and that they which see may become blind. Those of the Pharisees which were with him heard these things, and said unto him, Are we also blind? Jesus said unto them, If ye were blind, ye would have no sin: but now ye say, We see; your sin remaineth."

XXIII. (4) LOVE OF THE WORLD.

2 Tim. 4: 10: "For Demas forsook me, having loved this present world."

James 4: 3, 4: "Ye ask and receive not, because ye ask amiss, that ye may spend it in your pleasures. Ye adulteresses, know ye not that the friendship of the world is enmity with God?"

1 John 2: 15, 16, 17: "Love not the world, neither the things that are in the world. If any man love the world, the love of the Father is not in him. For all that is in the world, the lust of the flesh, and the lust of the eyes, and the vainglory of life, is not of the Father, but is of the world. And the world passeth away, and the lusts thereof: but he that doeth the will of God abideth forever."

XXIV. (5) LOVE OF MONEY.

Luke 16: 13-15: " No servant can serve two masters: for either he will hate the one and love the other; or else will hold to one and despise the other. Ye cannot serve God and mammon. And the Pharisees who are lovers of money heard all these things, and they scoffed at him. And he said unto them, Ye are they that justify yourselves in the sight of men;

but God knoweth your hearts: for that which is exalted among men is an abomination in the sight of God."

1 Tim. 6: 9, 10: " But they that desire to be rich fall into a temptation and a snare, and many foolish and hurtful lusts, such as drown men in destruction and perdition. For the love of money is a root of all kinds of evil: which some reaching after have been led astray from the faith and have pierced themselves through with many sorrows."

XXV. (6) CARES OF THE WORLD.

Luke 10: 40-42: "But Martha was cumbered about much serving; and she came up to him and said, Lord, dost thou not care that my sister did leave me to serve alone? Bid her therefore that she help me. But the Lord answered and said unto her, Martha, Martha, thou art anxious and troubled about many things: but one thing is needful: for Mary hath chosen the good part which shall not be taken away from her."

Matt. 13: 22: "And he that was sown

among the thorns, this is he that heareth
the word; and the care of the world, and
the deceitfulness of riches, choke the
word, and he becometh unfruitful.

XXVI. (7) DON'T WANT SINS EXPOSED.

Jno. 3: 19-21: "And this is the judgment, that the light is come into the
world, and men love the darkness rather
than the light; for their deeds were evil.
For every one that doeth ill hateth the
light, and cometh not to the light, lest
his works should be reproved. But he
that doeth the truth cometh to the light,
that his works may be made manifest,
that they have been wrought in God."

Prov. 28: 13: "He that covereth his
transgressions shall not prosper; but
whoso confesseth and forsaketh them
shall obtain mercy."

XXVII. (8) MURMURING SPIRIT.

Matt. 25: 24, 25, 29: "And he also that
had received the one talent came and said,
Lord, I knew thee that thou art a hard
man, reaping where thou didst not sow,

and gathering where thou didst not scatter: and I was afraid, and went away and hid thy talent in the earth: lo, thou hast thine own. For unto every one that hath shall be given, and he shall have abundance; but from him that hath not, even that which he hath shall be taken away."

PRAYER.

Our Father in Heaven, we thank Thee for Thy providence that saves and sustains. O grant that our souls may ever be upon their guard and the vigil-fires be lighted throughout the world, and we shall have victory through our Lord Jesus Christ.

SECTION F.

THE SELF-RIGHTEOUS.

You have often heard those who refuse to accept Christ urge, "I never did any thing bad." "I mean well." "I am good enough and better than a good many of the so-called Christians." "I don't think as you do." "Everybody has a

right to his own opinion." "I believe I
am right and am doing my best to be
saved." "I worship the God of nature,
and believe I will get to heaven." "It is
not necessary to be a church-member to
be saved." "I can go to heaven without
being baptized." "There are so many
denominations, I guess I am as near right
as any of you, anyhow."

A prodigious and indefinite amount of
sophistry, hypocrisy, bigotry, incompe-
tency, irrelevancy and iniquity can be run
in under expressions like the above.
These self-righteous and self-sufficient,
so-called "good, moral people," are
legion in number, but may generally be
sifted down into a struggle between self
and Christ.

O, if the soul would save itself, let it
find Christ and throw away self, "the old
man of sin!"

XXVIII. (1) DON'T WANT TO CONFESS
CHRIST.

Mark 8: 35: "For whosoever shall save
his life shall lose it; and whosoever shall

lose his life for my sake and the Gospel's shall save it."

Rom. 10: 9, 10: " Because if thou shalt confess with thy mouth Jesus as Lord, and shalt believe in thy heart that God raised him from the dead, thou shalt be saved, for with the heart man believeth unto righteousness; and with the mouth confession is made unto salvation."

Matt. 10: 32, 33: " Every one therefore who shall confess me before men, him will I also confess before my Father which is in heaven. But whosoever shall deny me before men, him will I also deny before my Father which is in heaven."

Jno. 14: 6: "Jesus saith unto him, I am the way and the truth and the life: no one cometh unto the Father, but by me."

Acts 4: 12: "And in none other is there salvation: for neither is there any other name under heaven, that is given among men, wherein we must be saved."

1 Jno. 5: 12: " He that hath the Son hath the life; he that hath not the Son of God hath not the life."

11

XXIX. (2) DON'T WANT TO BE BAPTIZED.

Mark 16: 16: "He that believeth and is baptized shall be saved: but he that disbelieveth shall be condemned."

Matt. 7: 21, 22: "Not every one that saith unto me, Lord, Lord, shall enter into the kingdom of heaven; but he that doeth the will of my Father which is in heaven. Many will say to me in that day, Lord, Lord, did we not prophesy by thy name, and by thy name cast out devils, and by thy name do many mighty works?"

Jno. 15: 10, 11: "If ye keep my commandments ye shall abide in my love, even as I have kept my Father's commandments, and abide in his love. These things have I spoken unto you, that my joy may be in you, and that your joy may be fulfilled."

Acts 2: 38: "And Peter said unto them, Repent ye, and be baptized every one of you in the name of Jesus Christ unto the remission of your sins; and ye shall receive the gift of the Holy Ghost."

Rom. 6: 4: "We were buried therefore with him through baptism into death: that like as Christ was raised from the dead through the glory of the Father, so we also might walk in newness of life."

PRAYER.

O our Father, we thank Thee for Thy great love. Grant that we may cheerfully follow these heaven-ordained ordinances; preserve them in their purity for us and our posterity, and not for us only, but for all who will receive them. We ask for Jesus' sake. Amen.

SECTION G.

MANY INFALLIBLE PROOFS FOR UNBELIEVERS.

There must be infallible proof of the truth of Christianity, because it is a religion of fact, not an expression of opinion. It was not done in an instant in some corner of the world, but claims to be an evolution of 6,000 years' duration, enacted

in the light places on every continent.
Thus assuming an historic form, it chal-
lenges investigation; indeed, any attempt
to hedge it about, while its devotees demand an unquestioning faith, is to remove
its facts into the region of the shadowy,
mysterious and unreal.

Each person, in some more or less independent way, should get at the historical facts and subject his faith to certain
tests, in order that he be not a victim of
fraud, mistake or superstition; thus can
he have an open-eyed confidence and a
boldness that is not bigotry.

Of course, in this section we can only
outline a consideration of evidences, with
the hope that such outline may be instrumental in assisting many to see their duty
of obedience to Christ, and seeing, per-
form; as, however, the soul may see and
yet not obey, so also the soul, through
ignorance or perversity, may not see, yet
the duty to obey remains.

You ask, How can this be? Notice,
one's responsibility is measured by his
opportunity to know what his duty is;

hence, the legal maxim, "Every man is presumed to know the law—ignorance is no excuse."

Industry and honesty cannot fail to lead the inquirer into the way of eternal life; these qualifications are humanity's two wings whereupon to rise to heaven; lose either, and the soul falls into sin or superstition.

XXX. (1) THEORIES OF INFIDELITY.

The sum of our faith is in Jesus Christ; he is the Alpha and the Omega of revelation—all time is focalized in him. His energies have wrought wonders in every land. "Jesus Hominum Salvator" is the universal creed of Christendom,—simple enough for a child, profound enough for a sage.

The real battle of infidelity rages around Jesus, for he is the "Gibraltar of Christian Evidences." If Christ was not as claimed and represented, infidels are called upon to account for him.

I. IMPOSTURE.

In an earlier age infidels who would not admit the claims of Jesus, reasoned that, whatever he was, he was no *fool*—he understood himself—he was an impostor. This theory is not accepted even by infidels in our day. Paine said, " He was a virtuous and amiable man." Ingersoll said, " For the man Christ I have the highest admiration and respect."

Could an impostor have (1) lived the purest life known to history? (2) Inaugurated a religion of beneficence and sublimity?

II. SELF-DECEPTION.

It is put forward by some infidels, as an explanation of Jesus, that he was self-deceived, that he imagined certain things of himself—was a fanatic, self-deluded, a visionary, a wild enthusiast. This theory is also denied by other infidels. Says one: " He was gifted with a grand, clear intellect, a perfectly balanced being." Renan said: " He represented the rare spectacle of a life, so far as we can estimate it, uniformly noble and consistent with his own lofty principles."

Jesus could not have been self-deceived, because of, (1) His practical precepts; (2) No taint of superstition appears in him; (3) He never magnified one truth at the expense of any other; (4) He was not deceived in either his disciples or others; (5) He never erred in judgment; (6) He taught men to control their religious enthusiasm, to think and to reflect.

III. NATURALISTIC.

The theory has been advanced that Jesus was not such an extraordinary man, after all, but a natural product, and that his disciples misunderstood, magnified and misrepresented his doings. "Jesus did not walk on the lake, but simply on the shores of the lake—but the eyes of the disciples deceived them. The eyes of the blind were healed by an efficacious eye-salve, but the *minutiæ* of the cure was not perceived by the disciples; that Jesus raised Lazarus and others, but only from a swoon," etc., etc.

This theory is in turn denied by other infidels. Strauss said: "This effort to get rid of the supernatural by a bold, realistic interpretation of the language of the Gospel narratives, whilst the credibility was represented in tact, was too glaring an outrage upon common sense to be successful."

This notion cannot be true: (1) It makes more difficulties than it solves; (2) The disciples themselves were too incredulous and slow of belief; (3) It would not comport with the teachings of Jesus; (4) Jesus especially guarded this point.

IV. MYTHICAL.

This theory, held by some infidels, is to the effect that round about Jesus are woven allegories, and fabulous statements of imaginary actions, etc.

This theory has not been generally approved by infidels. Chevalier Bunsen said: "The idea of men writing mythic histories between the time of Livy and Tacitus, and of Paul mistaking such for

realities!" "How can accounts which
are circumstantially correct in geography,
chronology, etc., be resolved into myths?"

It is much easier to believe in Jesus
than to believe that anyone could have
conceived and worked off such allegories
under the circumstances. Again, con-
temporaneous history will not warrant
such an assumption.

V. LEGENDARY.

This theory admits the early origin, authenticity and general veracity of the Gospel narrative, but that there was added
an unreality of the miraculous — that
Jesus consented to "play a part," disa-
greeable and distasteful, however; that
his miracles were "a violence done him
by his age—a concession which a pressing
necessity wrestled from him, and so he
entered on a course of *mild* and *beneficent*
deception."

A most remarkable theory this, and
other infidels will not accept such a self-
contradictory hypothesis. Holy fraud!
forsooth!

This theory cannot stand, because, (1)

Of the overwhelming evidence of the transcendent excellence of Jesus; (2) His attitude towards his disciples and the world was as leader, not as follower.

VI. ECLECTIC.

This theory is a combination of all the others, using here a little of one, and there some of the other. It maintains that Christianity is now superstition, now ignorance, now a fraud; that this is an allegory, and that a legend. So far short does this come from accounting for Jesus that it only confuses, beclouds and mystifies. It leaves us to wander in the night of agnosticism, closing all avenues of the soul to Him who is the "Light of the world."

PRAYER.

O our Heavenly Father, save us from the rank presumption that denies a high purpose and destiny for mankind, that denies the revelation Thou hast made of Thy will, and that involves us in the chaos and ruin of infidelity. O, as we prove the spirits, whether they be of Thee, may we not, in repudiating the counterfeit, cast off the true also. May we believe the evidence which Thou hast given of the true character of Thy only begotten Son, and confess that "Jesus Christ is come in the flesh." Help us in the power of Thy might to overcome the world with our great faith. We ask for Jesus' sake. Amen.

XXXI. (2) INTERNAL EVIDENCES.

The barest outline of evidence can be attempted here. The student is recommended, if possible, to pursue this line of study further; a number of good text books on Christian Evidences can be furnished by almost any bookseller.

By "internal evidences" of the truth of Christianity, we look at Christianity, as presented in the canon of the Scriptures, to see what marks of credibility, genuineness and authenticity it carries with itself. Notice, then:

I. PROPHECY.

"A miracle of knowledge," used to promote hope and faith. The prophecies of

Scripture are marked by, **(1)** worthy ends; **(2)** unambiguous language; **(3)** no failures of fulfillment; **(4)** a record preserved.

On the contrary, fraudulent prophecies and heathen oracles are, **(1)** unworthy; **(2)** ambiguous; **(3)** marked by failures; **(4)** leave no records.

(a) *Old Testament Prophecies.*—**(1)** Concerning the prosperity and adversity of the Israelites themselves; **(2)** the neighboring nations, as Tyre, Nineveh, Babylon, Egypt, etc.; **(3)** of the coming Messiah, his character, purposes and events in his life.

(b) *New Testament Prophecies and Fulfillment of Old Testament Prophecies.* —**(1)** Of the Jewish nation, siege, dispersion, unity, and peculiarities; **(2)** the life of Christ; **(3)** the prophecies of Christ, the destruction of Jerusalem, the inauguration and progress of the Kingdom of God.

The fulfillment of these prophecies is an ever-present miracle, testifying with over-powering weight to the genuineness, authenticity and credibility of the Christian Scriptures.

II. MIRACLES.

"Manifestations of superhuman power give authority to God's messengers," and are calculated to produce faith and obedience.

As contrasted with spurious miracles, Scriptural miracles are, (1) for important worthy purposes; (2) instantaneous and public; (3) sensible and easy to observe; (4) well authenticated.

III. HISTORICAL CONSIDERATION.

Notice the evidences afforded by the volume itself of, (1) the time covered; (2) the places mentioned; (3) the events narrated; (4) the character of the writers, as having an adequate knowledge of what they relate; (5) the remarkable preservation of the writings; the Hebrew and Greek languages uniquely fitted for this purpose; (6) the range of the Old and New Testament in these points present a most remarkable unity in diversity —a marvelous harmony without collusion.

This wonderful library of religious history contains within itself overwhelming evidence of being genuine, authentic and credible.

IV. CHARACTER OF JESUS.

The character of Jesus lends greatest weight to the credibility of Christianity; from his evident nature Jesus was without flaw. "I, having examined him before you, found no fault in this man." "Tempted, yet without sin." "No guile in his mouth." "Spake as never a man spake." "Teacher come from God, for no man can do these signs that thou doest, except God be with him." He was approved of God "by might, powers and wonders and signs, which God did by him in the midst of you, even as ye yourselves know." He was unjustly crucified; his judge said, "Behold, nothing worthy of death hath been done by him." He was raised from the dead, "nor did his flesh see corruption. This Jesus did God raise up, whereof we all are witnesses." He suffered and rose again from the dead, "and that repentance and remission of sins should be preached unto all nations, beginning from Jerusalem, ye are witnesses." His sympathies were with the poor, afflicted and down-trodden; all his life was consistent with these pure principles and holy purposes.

His was a revelation of the will of God perfected in man—a Divine human life—a perfect man!

V. THE CHARACTER ELECTED FOR HIS DISCIPLES.

No ostentatious almsgiving or prayers; no sanctimonious hypocrisy or meaningless ceremony; but meekness and purity, love of enemies, unfeigned fraternity. "Be perfect as your Father in heaven is perfect." "Except a man be born from above, he cannot see the kingdom of God, . . . that which is born of the flesh is flesh; and that which is born of the Spirit is spirit."

This feature of Christianity is absolutely unique. No religious faith, either adapted from Christianity or claiming originality, presents this remarkable aspect.

The sublimity of the elect Christian character is one of the strongest evidences of the credibility and genuineness of Christianity.

XXXII. (3) EXTERNAL EVIDENCES.

No one can reasonably deny, *a priori*, that the all-wise and all-powerful God can not only reveal his will, but can give to men a full and certain assurance that it is a true revelation.

I. THE NECESSITY.

The necessity for such revelation is apparent, because, (1) The ancient conceptions of the nature and the worship of God were dark, imperfect and monstrous; (2) Ignorance of the true genesis of the world; (3) Ignorance of the cause of depravity and misery among mankind; (4) Ignorance of the means of reconciliation between God and man; (5) There was no assurance of divine assistance towards the attainment and the perseverance in virtue; (6) No solid foundation for belief in the soul's immortality; (7) No adequate conception of the supreme felicity of man; (8) Only confused and monstrous notions concerning the rewards and punishments of a future state.

Christianity answers all these needs with absolute satisfaction.

II. CONTEMPORANEOUS HISTORY

Of Egyptian, Persian, Grecian and Roman life, where common points are touched, corroborates the Bible accounts.

The excavation of ancient ruins—coins, medals, monuments, etc., together with the reading of the symbolic languages of the ancients, give additional testimony to the accuracy, veracity and reliability of the Scriptures.

(a) *The Jews.*—The Jews, the city of Jerusalem, and the entire land of Palestine, from Christ's time till to-day, are mute and reluctant, but most remarkable witnesses of the credibility and authenticity of the Bible. (b) *Falsehood Detected.*—There is a moral certainty that Jewish leaders, such as Gamaliel and

12

Saul, would have detected and exposed falsehood and fraud concerning Jesus and the resurrection had such existed. (c) *Monuments.*—The ordinances instituted (baptism and the Lord's Supper) to perpetuate the principal facts and events of Christianity—observed to this day—are strong evidences of authenticity.

III. COMPARATIVE RELIGION.

The evidence of Christianity's divine origin and authority, as contrasted with other religions having admixtures of error and superstitions, is shown in, (1) Christianity's perfect concepts and precepts; (2) Its openness; (3) Its adaptation to the conditions and capacities of all mankind; (4) The spirituality of its worship; (5) Its opposition to the spirit of the world; (6) Its humiliation of man and exaltation of God; (7) Its restoration of order to the world; (8) Its contrariety to the covetousness and ambition of man; (9) Its eradication of evil passions from the heart; (10) Its restoring the divine image to man; (11) Its mighty effects in the governments of the world.

A CONVERTED LAWYER.

Tertullian, a converted lawyer, and called "the father of Latin Christianity," born A. D. 160, says in his able defense of the Christians, under the charge of being traitors to Rome, "That piety, veneration and loyalty, therefore, which is due emperors, does not consist in the fore-mentioned shows of duty, which even rebellion cloaks herself in, to pass undiscovered; but in such virtues as civil society finds necessary to be practiced sincerely towards prince and people. Nor are these actions of a virtuous mind looked upon by us as a tribute due to Cæsar only; for we have no respect of persons in doing good, because by so doing we do good to ourselves, who catch at no applause or reward from men, but from God only, who keeps a faithful register of our good works, and has ample rewards in store for this universal charity; for we have the same good wishes for emperors as for our nearest friends. To wish ill, to do ill, to speak ill, or to think ill of any one, we are equally forbidden without exception. What is injustice to an emperor, is injustice to his slave; and that which is unlawful against the meanest, is so against the greatest." And again, in defending the Christians against persecutions, Tertullian says: "But your reason is so entirely blinded with prejudice that you have not an eye left to see the public damage — a damage as visibly great as true. Not a man weighs what the common injury amounts to by thus depopulating the empire of the most just and innocent subjects in it; it is hardly credible to imagine how many Christian prisoners your judges destroy at every goal delivery, but only their trials are upon record.

"Among all this number of criminals, and this variety of indictments, what Christians do you find arraigned for assassinating, or for pickpockets, or for sacrilege, or for pilfering at the bath? Do you hear at the trials any article against Christians like that which other malefactors are charged withal? Do not the prisons sweat with your criminals continually? Do not the mines continually

groan with the load of heathens? Are
not your wild beasts fattened with heathens? And is not the whole herd of
condemned wretches, which some public
'benefactors' keep alive for the enter-
tainment of the amphitheater—are not
they all of your religion?

"Now, among all these malefactors,
there is not a Christian to be found for
any crime but that of his name only; or if
there be, we disown him for a Christian.

"We, then, are the only harmless people among you, and where is the wonder,
if it cannot well be otherwise? as in
truth it cannot, considering our education; for the innocence we are taught, we
are taught from God, and we know our
lesson perfectly well, as being revealed to
us by the Master of all perfection, and we
observe it faithfully as the command of
an All-seeing Lawgiver, whom we know
is not to be despised, but at the hazard
of eternal happiness. Whereas, your sys-
tems of doctrine are but the conjectures
of human philosophy, and the power
which commands obedience, merely hu-

man; and so neither the rule nor the power indisputable, and consequently the one too imperfect to instruct us fully, and the other too weak to command us effectually, both which (deficiencies) are abundantly provided for by revelation from God.

"Where is the philosopher who can so clearly demonstrate the true good as to fix the notion beyond dispute? And what human power is able to reach the conscience and bring down that notion into practice? For human wisdom is as subject to error as human power is to contempt.

"Therefore, let us enter a little more into a comparison between your laws and ours. Tell me, then, which do you take to be the fullest and completest law, that which says thou shalt do no murder, or that which resists the very passion of anger? Which expresses greatest purity and perfection, the law which prohibits the outward act of adultery, or that which condemns the bare lust of the eye? Which is the wisest provision for innocence, to forbid evil doing, or not to permit so much as evil speaking? Which is the most instructing lesson for the good of mankind, to debar men from doing injury, or not so much as to allow the injured person the common privilege of returning evil for evil?

"But this is not all, for I must give you to understand that these very laws of yours, which are but in the way to perfection, are no more in good truth than a transcript of the old law of God, older by much than any law of your making; but I have already laid before you the antiquity of Moses."

Thus far the reliable Tertullian and in view of the history intervening, and of the remarkable fact that seven-eighths of the world's territory is to-day under Christian governmental control, who can doubt that our "faith is the victory that overcomes the world."

PRAYER.

. O our Father, hasten the day when animosities and wars and corruptions in

high and low places shall disappear, and
all shall be thine in Christ Jesus our
Lord, to whom be glory and honor and
power. World without end. Amen.

www.ingramcontent.com/pod-product-compliance
Lightning Source LLC
Chambersburg PA
CBHW020536270326
41927CB00006B/602